WORDSMITHING

The Art & Craft of Writing for Public Relations

Ron Rhody & Carol Ann Hackley

PEARSON

Custom
Publishing

Printed in the United States of America

10 9 8 7 6 5 4 3 2 1

ISBN 0-536-12277-6

2005420432

MT/JW

Please visit our web site at *www.pearsoncustom.com*

PEARSON CUSTOM PUBLISHING
75 Arlington Street, Suite 300, Boston, MA 02116
A Pearson Education Company

CONTENTS

CHAPTER THREE

The Professional's Code of Conduct: A Matter of Ethics   16

UNIT TWO

The Basics: The Forms, Formulas and Uses of the Various Types of Releases   21

CHAPTER FOUR

The Five Ws and the Fwsh: Formulas for Writing Effective Copy   23

CHAPTER FIVE

What Makes a Story?   30

CHAPTER SIX

Getting the Information You Need   33

CHAPTER SEVEN

The Five Types of Releases and How to Write Four of Them   37

CHAPTER EIGHT

A Step-By-Step Template for Constructing a Release, from the Lead to Clearances and Distribution   50

CHAPTER NINE

Targeting: Getting to the Right People with the Right Message   59

UNIT THREE

Beyond the Basics: Pieces that Sell, Persuade, Inform and Motivate   63

CHAPTER TEN

Op-Ed Pieces, Signed Articles and Letters as Tactical Tools   65

CHAPTER ELEVEN

Conventional Letters, Newsletters and Brochures   76

CHAPTER TWELVE

Media Kits and Fact Sheets   83

CHAPTER THIRTEEN

Writing for Radio and TV: News, Features and PSAs   93

CHAPTER FOURTEEN

Position Papers and Formal Statements   102

CHAPTER FIFTEEN

Briefing Papers and Q&As   112

CHAPTER SIXTEEN

Pitches and Précis: Selling Story Ideas   121

CHAPTER SEVENTEEN

Writing for the Internet   125

CHAPTER EIGHTEEN

Writing for Crisis Management and Damage Control Situations   128

CHAPTER NINETEEN

Writing Speeches   134

CHAPTER TWENTY

Writing for the Internal Constituency   147

UNIT FOUR

Et Cetera: Special Words and Special Readings 157

FOREWORD

Authors' Note

Wordsmithing is about the *how* and *why* of writing for public relations. It is intended for people who are serious about being public relations professionals. Its emphasis, therefore, is on the *essentials* of the *fundamental skill* required to become a professional—the ability to write clearly and persuasively.

RELEASES FIRST, FOLLOWED BY THE MORE DEMANDING FORMS

The first part of the book places heavy emphasis on releases, which have long been considered the bread and butter of the craft. The basic types of releases, the standard formats used for each, how to write them, and the uses for which they are intended, are covered in detail. A special section on grammar and spelling is also included. The lessons therein can be applied throughout the course and should be kept handy for ready reference.

Following releases, the book covers the more challenging and advanced writing forms that play a key role in all programs that inform, persuade or enlist support for the achievement of a specific goal. Other forms include white papers, op-ed pieces, speeches, by-liners, statements and position papers, reports, letters and memos, to name a few.

Also included are sections on writing for the internal audience and on the writing forms and considerations involved with crisis management and damage control. Crisis management, after all, is one of the most important and increasingly prevalent challenges facing today's public relations professionals.

Each chapter ends with a set of interactive exercises that are included on the CD found at the back of the text. Each exercise presents a public relations problem for which you are asked to offer a solution. You may view our solutions or suggestions, and compare your results.

We have not tried to cover all the forms of writing for public relations. Other forms such as script writing for promotional videos, for instance, or advertising copy in support of issues or positioning, or the nuances of producing posters and slogans sometimes essential to certain programs are not covered here. Our focus instead is on the essential forms every public relations professional is expected to know and handle effectively.

AS MUCH ATTENTION TO THE *WHY* OF THINGS AS TO THE *HOW*

In all instances, considerable attention is devoted to the *why* of things—to the strategies and tactics involved in the creation and use of all the key forms. Understanding the reason you're writing something is as important as knowing how to perform the technical aspects of the function.

Examples of each of the writing forms discussed in the text will be found in the body of the appropriate chapter, at its end, or on the CD-ROM.

We can't state strongly enough that one of the most effective ways to learn how to write is to write a lot, write some more, and rewrite what you've written. In that spirit, the book contains exercises at the end of each chapter to give you experience with this very necessary practice. Don't forget we also learn to write by reading a lot. Some suggested readings are also noted.

A CONVERSATIONAL AND INFORMAL STYLE

We have tried to make this text as readable and interesting as possible by using an informal approach and conversational tone, and by keeping the discussion of each topic as concise as possible, while covering all the essentials. We hope you find the result clearly understandable and "user friendly."

A WORD ABOUT "WORDSMITHING"

Wordsmiths are craftsmen, who, like goldsmiths and silversmiths, create works of real utility. Goldsmiths and silversmiths use precious metals. Wordsmiths use words. In either case, when it's done well, it's pure artistry.

AND A PROGNOSTICATION

Finally, those of you who are embarking on your careers in this opening decade of the 21st century are in for what ought to be one of the most exciting and rewarding periods the profession has experienced. Without doubt, it will be among the most challenging. Your opportunities to do important work and be well-compensated, while reaping great personal satisfaction, are limited only by your ambition and your talent. We wish you luck.

OVERVIEW: CONTEXT AND FUNDAMENTALS

## CHAPTER ONE

A BRIEF OVERVIEW OF THE PUBLIC RELATIONS FUNCTION AND WRITING'S ROLE THEREIN

Writing is the basic tool of public relations.

Notice that the word is *the*, not *a.* To be effective in the field, the public relations professional must use and understand many types of tools. However, writing is *the most important* and powerful tool.

Why?

We must be able to communicate effectively in order to work together, whether it is to build families, companies or nations.

We must be able to communicate intelligently to gain knowledge and share information, whether to drive a car, map DNA or settle border disputes.

We must be able to communicate imaginatively to define and deliver the ideas and the ideals that sustain cultures and advance civilization.

If we can't or don't communicate, we won't succeed—person-to-person, company-to-company or nation-to-nation.

Communication is the quintessential human skill. It is also the quintessential management skill. And writing is the key to effective communication.

This is so, because writing is the one discipline that forces us to think clearly about what we want to impart, to choose the words and information that best describe what we mean in terms our targets can identify with and understand, and then to package our message in the phrases and imagery that will deliver the idea, emotion or fact we want conveyed in the most persuasive and memorable way.

When we write, we are forced to be focused, disciplined and thoughtful. It's with writing that we have the best chance of successfully making our case, even if what we want to communicate is to be heard, not read.

Words and ideas that cause action, motivate, inform and move are rarely the result of off-the-cuff comments or ad-lib reactions. They are crafted. They are polished and sharpened and refined. They become instruments. They are written in a specific way to achieve a specific end. That's what writing for public relations is all about.

Public relations is a management discipline that, if applied correctly, can affect what people know, how they think and, ultimately, how they act. The function puts major emphasis on building and maintaining relationships, and on informing and educating—all with the ultimate objective of affecting behavior. Its principal instrument is communications and its single most important tool is writing.

CREATING, PACKAGING AND MARKETING IDEAS

Regardless of the type of organization, the public relations function has certain qualities in common. First and foremost is an expertise in the uses of the tools and techniques of mass and interpersonal communications. It typically features a corps of creative people constantly looking for new ways to draw attention to and sustain interest in products and services, and who also have the skill to phrase, package and deliver ideas that advance the organization's interests. Experts in crisis management, damage control, community relations and employee communications usually are part of the group as well. Without exception, the public relations function has responsibility for media relations.

There are six unique ways the public relations function helps an organization reach its goals:

1. It creates support from employees and fosters a sense of team by building understanding of what the organization is trying to achieve, and how they benefit from helping it reach its goals. (Employee or internal communications)
2. It promotes and enhances public understanding around issues and actions, allows the public, lawmakers, and regulators to be supportive of the organization, and develops and manages the persuasive presentation of the organization's case to its key governmental and regulatory officials and their staffs. (Governmental or public affairs)
3. For profit-making organizations, it draws attention to and creates interest in products and services in direct support of the marketing effort, and in not-for-profit organizations, it works to support funding and service objectives. (Marketing support communications and product publicity)
4. It anticipates potential problems before they become major issues and identifies strategies and tactics to defuse such situations. If a crisis is already in progress, it takes the actions necessary to mitigate the impact. (Crisis management and damage control)
5. It provides an interface with the media that generates reasonable attention to the company's achievements and encourages fair and balanced reporting in times of trouble. (Media relations)
6. It establishes and maintains a positive interface with key stakeholders and audiences, manages the organization's good citizen and good neighbor reputations, and often serves as an ombudsman for community interests. (Community relations)

This is not an exhaustive list of the function's scope. Financial communications, corporate advertising, corporate philanthropy, opinion research, etc. are often part of the portfolio. But those mentioned in detail are certainly core responsibilities.

Public Relations is a thinking game. It is about creating, packaging and marketing ideas. Ideas are useless until and unless they can be articulated so others can react to them, use them or buy into them. For an idea to be articulated effectively, it has to be written—even if its final form is the spoken word.

This is the primary reason the first question typically asked of most entry-level candidates seeking positions in public relations is, "Can you write?"

Anyone with reasonable intelligence, a high school-level vocabulary, the ability and willingness to read, access to a dictionary and the determination to work at it can become a good writer. This book's mission is to help you on your way.

THE BASIC FORMS OF WRITING FOR PUBLIC RELATIONS

When you have finished this book, you should have a solid grasp of the basic forms of writing for public relations, along with a firm understanding of where, how, when and why to use each form.

The basic forms are:

1. Releases—which come in a variety of guises
2. Feature stories
3. Signed articles
4. Op-ed pieces and letters
5. Statements and positions papers
6. Fact Sheets, FAQs and Q&As
7. Memos
8. Speeches
9. Story pitches
10. Program writing
11. Writing for crisis management and damage control
12. Writing for employee audiences

As mentioned in the *Foreword*, the first truth about writing is that while the basics can be taught, the only true way to learn to write well is to write—a lot. The second truth is that we learn to write by reading—a lot. Osmosis works. You don't have to read articles covering theory or scholarly tomes. Read purely for the enjoyment of the written word, about things that may catch your imagination. Keep an eye out for good writers whose approach might give you some ideas.

There is a final point to be made here at the beginning and kept in mind: *Different from any other kind of writer, the public relations professional is a player, not a spectator.* He or she isn't sitting on the sidelines, observing and reporting, but is a participant, actively involved with what is happening and helping to shape outcomes.

This is a role not to be taken lightly.

INTERACTIVE EXERCISES CHAPTER 1

A Brief Overview of the Public Relations Function and Writing's Role Therein

Exercise One
Three key points in this opening chapter are: (A) why writing is important in the practice of public relations, (B) the working definition of public relations used for the purposes of this book, and (C) why public relations writing is different from other forms of writing. Write a short article covering these three points, using this

book as the authority and aimed at readers of your student newspaper. At this point you have had no exposure to writing releases, so write the article in whatever way you think might be most interesting to your intended audience. Hold on to this. We'll compare it with the way you handle the same subjects at the end of this book.

Exercise Two

Below are the lead paragraphs of three stories that were released by business corporations. We haven't discussed this in any detail yet, but try to identify which qualifies as hard news, which as a product release, and which as a feature.

A. Ft. Lauderdale, Fla.—For anyone who has ever had to cut short a nighttime outdoor event when the sun went down, now there is an alternative. Vector Manufacturing, Ltd., a leading developer of consumer-friendly portable power products, has come out with a new line of rechargeable patio lamps that provide illumination for up to eight hours on a standard household charge.

B. New York, NY—Its doors have been shut for exactly a year but tomorrow (Sept. 11) at noon, Brooks Brothers will reopen its lower Manhattan story at One Liberty Plaza. Severely damaged by the terrorist attacks that resulted in the collapse of the World Trade Center, the store is one of the first in the area to come back into full operation.

C. Los Angeles, Calif.—The Los Angeles County Museum of Art announced today plans for a $30 million expansion of its California Heritage wing. The expansion, to be completed in 2006, is being financed by a $15 million grant from an anonymous donor and a matching amount from Los Angeles County.

Use the CD-ROM to compare your responses to our suggested answers.

## CHAPTER TWO

WRITE IT RIGHT: A SHORT PRIMER ON GRAMMAR AND SPELLING

The ABCs of writing for PR are *Accuracy, Brevity* and *Clarity.* Simple errors in spelling, punctuation and grammar—carelessness with facts, or worse, "facts" that are not factual—kill credibility and destroy trust. They also mark the author as lazy, uneducated, stupid, or all of the above. No one can win friends for a cause or influence people to a particular way of thinking bearing such a handicap. So, write it right.

The following examples of misuses, miscues, errors and misunderstandings represent a collection of the most common mistakes made by students in public relations classes throughout our collective 25-plus years of teaching. Consider them carefully.

SPELLING DEMONS (A.K.A. WORDS OFTEN SPELLED INCORRECTLY)

Although there are many "spelling demons," a few stand out as being the most prevalent. Be especially aware of them! Make a rule to always double-check your writing, and do not depend on the computer's spell-checking function. When the first "L" is left out of "public relations," your spell check will tell you the word is correct. It is, of course, but it's probably not aligned with your intended meaning. "The L from hell" can spell disaster and embarrassment for the negligent proofreader.

Common usage seemingly contributes to the violation of rules of spelling and grammar, as through the years our spoken language has deteriorated by adoption of an "everybody's using it" philosophy. However, there are good reasons for sticking to proper English, most especially your credibility and that of your organization.

The following tips will help you raise a "red flag" and check spelling:

- a lot: two separate words (*not* "alot")
- all right: meaning correct or OK (*not* "alright")
- accommodate: (note: two Ms)
- adviser: preferred spelling, although "advisor" also is correct
- cannot: all one word
- desert: dry and arid, like the Sahara!
- dessert: remember, you'd rather have more "dessert" than "desert"—so double the "s" for a sweet treat.

- divulge: to reveal
- flyer: preferred spelling for "brochure," although "flier" also is correct
- Governor: do not forget the first "r."
- hors d'oeuvres: appetizers
- receive: your elementary school teacher said, "It's 'i' before 'e,' except after 'c,' or when sounded as 'a' as in 'neighbor' or 'weigh.'" Of course, there are a few exceptions.
- separate: (note: "ar," not "er")

HOMONYMS: THEY SOUND THE SAME BUT AREN'T

Watch out for homonyms, those words that sound the same, but are spelled differently and have different meanings. Examples include:

- ad: advertisement (remember, by the way, that ads are printed, commercials are broadcast)
- add: addition (i.e., 2 + 2 = 4)
- capital: the city, money or capital letter
- capitol: legislative building
- dam: holds back water
- damn: expletive! (swear word)
- foreword: opening section, the "fore"-"word" (the word that comes before)
- forward: a direction, as in "Forward march!"
- moose: Very large four-legged animal, found in such places as Alaska
- mouse: a rodent
- mousse: a whipped dessert (don't mix up "moose," "mouse" or "mousse," or we won't want to dine at your house!)
- principal: the main or major component, or the head of a school
- principle: the premise or rule (note that it ends in "le," like "rule")
- roomers: people who live in a boarding house
- rumors: that which is spread through the grapevine (not all of which is true)
- stationary: (key: "a"—to remain in pl*a*ce; e.g., "P.J.'s desk is stationary.")
- stationery: (key: "e"—to use with a p*e*n; e.g., "Kim chose blue stationery for her thank-you note.")
- to = preposition
- too = also or excessively (e.g., "He, too, was hurt in the accident." "She was too ill to attend.")
- two = number
- their: possessive plural pronoun
- there: place
- they're: the contraction for "they are"
- you're: the contraction for "you are"
- your: second person, possessive (e.g., "Your article is well written.")

PROPER NOUNS

There's no excuse for misspelling a proper noun. Contracts and clients have been lost and reputations have been ruined because of such errors. Case in point: One PR firm spent bundles on a presentation hoping to land a particularly lucrative contract. But, when the leather-bound portfolio of materials was handed to the CEO with his misspelled name embossed in gold on the cover, he exclaimed, "No company will handle our account, if it can't spell my name correctly!"

Assuming a word to the wise is sufficient, *check all proper nouns.* It's easy to do. You can research proper spellings in phonebooks, atlases, annual reports, library and business research sources, and the Internet.

Among the most frequently misspelled proper nouns are the following:

· Marriott: hotel chain
· Men's Wearhouse: "I guarantee it!"—men's store
· JCPenney: the store, all one word (not penny, the one-cent piece)
· Procter & Gamble: consumer products corporation
· Berkeley, Calif.
· Colombia: South American country
· Columbia: University, or Washington, District of Columbia
· Houston, Texas
· Los Angeles, Calif.
· Pittsburg, Calif.
· Pittsburgh, Penn.
· San Francisco, Calif.

PRONOUN PROBLEMS

One of the most frequent difficulties encountered in writing occurs when pairing nouns and pronouns. A few suggestions will help clarify *proper* usage:

· A singular subject *requires* a singular pronoun: (e.g., "The employee . . . he [or she] [or his or her] . . ." or "The company . . . it [or its]")
· A plural subject requires a plural pronoun: (e.g., "The employees . . . they [or their]")
· No matter how long the name, a company is singular: The Company = it (singular) (e.g., "The Cusick, Hall & Floyd Co. scheduled its annual meeting in Hawaii"; "Johnson & Johnson handled its crisis extremely well.")

Note: all of the following are singular and require the singular pronoun—his or her, *not* their. (For example, "Everyone must buy *his or her* own lunch" is correct . . . not "*their* lunch.")

· anyone = his or her
· everyone = his or her
· no one = his or her
· someone = his or her
· anybody = his or her
· everybody = his or her
· nobody = his or her
· somebody = his or her

MEDIA OR MEDIUM? AND ANOTHER LATIN STICKLER

- media: channels of communication, plural (e.g., "The media were invited.")
- medium: channel of communication, singular (e.g., "Television is the medium of choice . . ."), or a clairvoyant
- alumni: plural
- alumna: female singular
- alumnus: male singular
- alumnae: female plural

REFLEXIVE PRONOUNS

Be careful when using reflexive pronouns, such as "myself, yourself, herself, himself, itself and themselves." Use these only when action is happening to the subject. For example, "I hurt myself" or, "The children organized themselves into teams." But never: "Join my family and myself in celebrating graduation." Rather, it is, "Join my family and me in celebrating graduation." (To test for pronouns, eliminate the noun. For example, shorten the sentence above to "Join . . . me in celebrating." It would never be "Join *myself* in celebrating!" The test works!)

APOSTROPHES

Apostrophes seem to creep into sentences where none are needed. Be sure you understand the purpose of the apostrophe: to indicate the possessive or to take the place of a missing letter in a contraction.

- Apostrophe as part of contraction: replaces the missing letter (aren't = are not; doesn't = does not; can't = cannot)
- It's and its are frequently misused: it's = contraction for "it is" (it *never* means anything else); its = possessive (and *its'* is *never* correct)
- Possessive pronouns, such as yours, ours, his, hers, its and theirs, have no apostrophe.
- Unless it's possessive, the "s" on the end of an acronym does not need an apostrophe (for example, it's Q&As, not Q&A's).
- Apostrophe showing possession:
    - lady's = singular possessive
    - ladies' = plural possessive
    - woman's = singular possessive
    - women's = plural possessive
    - child's = singular possessive
    - children's = plural possessive
    - bird's = singular possessive
    - birds' = plural possessive
    - Patrick's = possessive

Note: The apostrophe follows the base word. If the base word ends with an "s" and the usage is plural, then the apostrophe follows the "s." Otherwise, the "s" follows the apostrophe. If the word is plural, such as "children," but does not end in "s," then add an apostrophe and an "s."

"COULD OF"—OUCH!

Although slurred speech makes it sound like people are saying "could of" or "would of" or "should of," it is really "could've," "would've," and "should've" for "could have," "would have," and "should have" (e.g., "I could've had a V-8" is the short version for "I could have had a V-8.").

A FEW THOUGHTS ON PUNCTUATION

- Use commas to separate items in a series, except just before "and." ("The decorations were red, white and blue.")
- Use commas and semicolons when dividing complicated materials, such as names and titles. ("We elected Alexis, president; Kimberly, vice president; Michelle, treasurer, and Leah, secretary.") Switch from semicolon to comma, just before the "and."
- Use a semicolon before "however" and comma afterwards, when it is used as a conjunction. ("She came home for the holidays; however, she could not stay long.")
- The same rule applies to "therefore." ("He flunked the test; therefore, he will take it again.")
- In other instances, use commas to set off "however" and "therefore." ("She, however, was stunned by his silence" or "I, therefore, listened attentively.")
- Use a comma to separate independent clauses, joined by a conjunction (and, but, for, or, nor, because or so). ("I called you, because . . .")
- In a compound sentence, use a comma before the conjunction. ("The students studied together, and they passed the test!" "The student knew the material, but he could not answer the questions.")
- Use a comma in direct address: "Professor, I need your help."
- Use commas to set off geographical addresses. ("Kevin was born in Columbus, Ohio, but now lives in Reno, Nevada.")
- Use quotation marks to indicate inclusion of someone's exact words. (The teacher asked, "Do you like to write?")
- Use a comma after an "if-phrase." ("If you need my help, let me know.") And, when using "if," remember to use the verb "were," not "was." ("If I were in your shoes, I would call home for help." "If this were July, we would be swimming!")
- Use a comma after "for example." ("For example, he gained 50 pounds.")
- Use a hyphen as follows: 13-year-old girl; 30-second commercial; one-minute break; 15-page paper; three-day cruise; 24-hour hotline; king-size bed.
- Use exclamation points sparingly. Normally you should use a period or question mark to end a sentence; otherwise you'll sound breathless.
- Quotation marks go outside other punctuation. ("I enjoy teaching," she said. "I created this guide to help you.")
- Underline all publication names or use italics.

WATCH YOUR WORDS

Do not repeat *key* words in the same sentence. This rule alone will eliminate wordiness and awkwardness (e.g., "The *University* of Hawaii students have been attending *University* classes for two weeks." Eliminate the second "University"). Check all of your copy for this common type of redundancy.

- Go on a "*which*" hunt when you edit your writing. Eliminate unnecessary "which" and "that"; they clutter your copy.
- And speaking of "that," when you do use it, make sure your usage is correct:
    People = Who ("The officers, who were elected in May . . .")
    Things = That ("The company that created the new product . . .")
    Remember: "Chevron was the company that . . . ," but "Tom and Janet are the psychologists who . . ."
- "Effect" or "affect"? Generally, "effect" is the noun; "affect" is the verb. ("The effect of the Berlin Wall was . . ." or "The fall of the Berlin Wall affected many." An exception is: "Betty was able to effect a change.")
- "Less" or "fewer?" Use "less" when it is an amount that can be measured (e.g., "less flour," "less sugar"), but "fewer" when the noun can be counted (e.g., "fewer members," "fewer flowers"). An easy way to remember is to "use fewer eggs, and less sugar."
- Beware the pitfalls of loose, lose, loss:
    Loose = Adjective ("The loose button on her sweater . . .")
    Lose = Verb ("If I lose my only set of keys . . .")
    Loss = Noun ("The loss of his job . . .")

NUMBERS

- Spell out single-digit numbers (nine and below); use figures for numbers 10 and higher, except when a sentence begins with a number, or in money, age and dates. (e.g., "Denny weighed nine pounds at birth." "The Professor has 35 students in class." "William, 6, was born December 17." "John gave her $5." "The project was estimated to cost $1.5 million.")
- When dealing with money, follow the generally accepted pattern of omitting the decimal point when the amount is even: ($25, not $25.00). It's too easy to misplace a decimal point in print, changing the meaning dramatically. Use "$1," not "one dollar."
- In writing amounts with multiple zeroes, use the word "million" or "billion," as in "$1.2 million," "$2 billion." Again, it's the possibility of dropping a zero that dictates this rule.
- When using the "$" symbol, it's redundant to also use the term "dollars." (e.g., "The budget for the project is $1.5 million," NOT "The total cost of the effort was $1.5 million dollars.")
- Spell out a numeral when it is the first word in a sentence. (e.g., "Twenty-three elephants escaped." "Eleven students were invited to Ben's party.")

DATES AND TIMES

- Always organize your information by time, date, and place (e.g., "The event is to be held at 11 a.m., Friday, May 13, in the Smith Room of the Peyton Hotel.")
- When writing the current date, do not use the year. It's obvious (e.g., "Emily will graduate June 19.")
- If you are writing about a previous year, or one to come, use the numbers. Otherwise, leave out the year (e.g., "Kim graduated May 14, 1994.")

"NEWS" RELEASES—SAYS, SAID AND GOT

- News release is the preferred term, because it encompasses all forms of media. Only one medium uses a printing press and "press" releases. Don't risk insulting the electronic media.
- Use "said," *not* "says" in interviews and when quoting someone (e.g., "It's important," he said.)
- Use "says," when referring to a printed document or sign (e.g., "The ad says the new model Palm Pilots are available . . ." "The Bible says . . .")
- Although AOL's online voice exclaims, "You've Got Mail!" and the popular ad campaign asks, "Got milk?," eliminate the use of "got." Rely on "have" instead.
- Always capitalize official titles when used before names; titles are only lower case when following a name. (e.g., "According to Chief School Administrator Robert Doyle . . ." "Robert Doyle, chief school administrator, said today . . .")

TIPS FOR WRITING LEADS

- Keep the lead paragraph short: a maximum of 25 words is a good rule of thumb. While reporters for *The New York Times* do not count the words in their leads, those learning to write professionally will do well to make sure their leads do not exceed the recommended maximum number.
- Avoid starting the lead paragraph with the day, date or time. Rarely is that aspect of the story the most interesting. (Only do so if that's the most important fact: "May 18 is the new date for graduation.")
- Also, avoid starting the lead with a person's name, unless that individual is a "household word," or a celebrity, whose every action is of interest to the reading public. For example, "President George W. Bush choked on a pretzel today" would be appropriate, while "Jane Smith choked on a pretzel today" would not. In the second instance, the reporter would write, "A local high school teacher, Jane Smith, choked on a pretzel . . . ," to identify the category of the individual ("high school teacher") and localize it for the interest of readers. It was obviously a "slow news" day.

OTHER NO-NOs

- "In regard to" (not "In *regards* to")
- "Toward" (not "Towards")
- "Often" (not "Often times")
- Never use "each and every," That's drippy and redundant!
- Never say, "Please RSVP." That's also redundant. RSVP is *repondez s'il vous plait,* which means "please respond" in French.
- Eliminate excess verbiage to keep copy tight (e.g., "canary bird." A canary *is* a bird. "Easter Sunday." Easter is always on Sunday.)
- Always use "try to," not "try *and*" (e.g., "Try *to* enjoy the play," not "Try *and* enjoy the play.")
- "Emphasis" is the noun; "emphasize" is the verb.
- "Enthusiastic" is the adjective. "Enthusiasm" is the noun.
- "Both are" is plural (e.g., "Both students are presenting their projects.")

- "Each was" is singular (e.g., "Each of the women was voicing her own opinion.")
- "Neither is" is always singular (e.g., "Neither woman is willing to volunteer her time.")
- "Neither was" is also singular (e.g., "Neither boy was willing to share his toy.")
- Do not split a paragraph in a news release from one page to another. Complete the paragraph on one page.
- Do not split verbs (e.g., "The girl already has seen the movie," not "The girl has already seen the movie.")
- Keep construction parallel. When using the "-ing" form in a list, be consistent; when using past tense, be consistent (e.g., "Alex enjoys walking, swimming, dancing and golfing." "During our vacation, we biked, hiked and golfed.")
- "Moral" or "morale?" "That's the moral of the story," but "Staff morale is low." (Hopefully, staff members are moral!)
- "Rational" or "rationale?" "The rational human being would . . . ," but "The rationale for the decision . . ."
- Make sure subjects and verbs agree. A singular noun requires a singular verb and pronoun. (e.g., "The boy ran around his house." Singular noun: "boy"; singular verb: "ran"; singular pronoun: "his." "The girls ran around their houses." Plural noun: "girls"; plural verb: "ran"; plural pronoun: "their.")
- Do not end a sentence with a preposition. (Not: "That is the man he spoke with," but "That is the man with whom he spoke." And never: "Where are you at?" but "Where are you?"). Prepositions are words such as: with, at, up, through, to, under, above, around and about.

Words are jewels. String them together carefully to convey meaning, inform, educate, persuade and inspire. Choose them thoughtfully. Use them artfully. Poor workmanship spoils the gem.

INTERACTIVE EXERCISE CHAPTER 2

Write It Right: A Short Primer on Grammar and Spelling

Exercise One

This chapter covered common errors that are easy to make and are made far too frequently. Avoiding them is mostly a matter of paying attention to the intended meaning of the word and to a reasonable understanding of the basic rules of grammar. These are rules with which all should be familiar. Based on the material contained in this chapter, test your understanding by correcting the following sentences. Compare your corrections with the correct answers that follow:

1. I can not come to the meeting on Friday.
2. The stationary was on sale!
3. The company issued their Annual Report.
4. No one had their assignment ready to turn in.
5. The tree lost it's leaves.
6. "If I was living in New York, I'd attend plays regularly!"
7. The teacher gave a three hour examination to his' students before spring brake.
8. The program was discontinued, because the program funds were unavailable.
9. Marylea was the one that accepted the position for night duty.
10. The company hired people that had the appropriate credentials.
11. Less students enrolled for Spring semester.
12. She enjoyed golf, skiing and swimming.
13. Be sure to ask your guests to please RSVP by March 1.
14. I will try and come to the event.
15. You can also plan to take the course next semester.
16. The rational for the decision was clear to me.
17. "Where are you at?"
18. He said the project would cost one million dollars.
19. He estimated the new building would require an additional $10,500,000.
20. Have you ever shopped at the new J.C. Penny store, near the Mariott in Berkley?
21. I bought a plane ticket to Columbia in South America, but wound up in Columbia, Missouri!
22. Everyone is required to register their car, before obtaining a parking permit.
23. He bought an add in the Sunday magazine.
24. The media was notified of the press conference.
25. The young man said, "Please join my family and myself for graduation on Saturday."

Use the CD-ROM to check your answers.

## CHAPTER THREE

THE PROFESSIONAL'S CODE OF CONDUCT: A MATTER OF ETHICS

Ethics are like virginity. You only lose them once. Never compromise your ethics, or bend to the whims of others to please a boss or client. Always protect your credibility and professional standing.

Ethical conduct is the bedrock on which reputations are built. Nothing is as important as you embark on your career as your understanding of the ethical principles that drive your actions. You have a commitment to honoring those principles, regardless of outside pressures.

From your first days on earth, you have been bombarded with messages from a variety of influences that shape your morals and values. Entire books, courses of study, expensive seminars, training sessions, sensitivity retreats—a veritable ethics industry—are devoted to the subject. What we address here cannot begin to cover all the current rhetoric about ethics. Instead, we will concentrate on what is meant by ethical conduct as defined for and by public relations professionals.

We should be clear on our terms. Webster's Dictionary defines ethics as: 1. the principles of honor and morality; 2. accepted rules of conduct; 3. the moral principles of an individual. The public relations profession has a well-defined set of ethical principles governing conduct. We'll come to those shortly, We'll start with a few general comments about trying to do what's right by operating ethically.

One of the simplest, and best, statements of ethical conduct is "The Cadet's Code." It says: "A Cadet does not lie, cheat or steal—or tolerate people who do." There is nothing ambiguous, slithery or tentative in this statement. We recommend it as a guide. It will serve you well.

There is nothing very complicated about acting ethically. Many of the choices can be tough, because they almost always involve greed or self-interest. But most of the time, most of us know the right answer. Most of us had a pretty good idea of the difference between right and wrong by the time we were in the sixth grade. Problems arise when we don't want to do what we know is right, when we want to find a way to avoid doing it, or we attempt to rationalize our way around it.

Difficulties occur when we to try balance what we know is right against what our peers or our organizations expect of us, or when we want something badly enough to let that desire override our otherwise good sense. When that happens, our own inner voice gets muffled and we acquiesce to things we would not otherwise accept.

THE PERILS OF GROUP THINK

When we become victims of "group think," we can be seduced into unethical actions by peer pressure and the rationalization that "it's legal, isn't it?" Just because something is legal doesn't mean that it's the ethical course of action. Courage and character are required to recognize and resist being drawn into these traps. You must be alert. As stated in the introduction to this chapter—and it bears repeating—ethics are like virginity. You only lose them once.

Let's move to the standards of ethical practice expected of public relations professionals.

THE PRSA CODE

The Public Relations Society of America (PRSA) has a formal Code of Professional Standards all members are expected to follow, and that serve as a guideline for the entire profession, whether the player is a PRSA member or not.

The PRSA Code instructs members to:

- Preserve the integrity of the process of communication;
- Be honest and accurate in all communications;
- Act promptly to correct erroneous communications for which the practitioner is responsible, and
- Preserve the free flow of unprejudiced information when giving or receiving gifts, by ensuring that gifts are nominal, legal and infrequent.

The code lists the following core principles:

- *Free flow of information.* Protecting and advancing the free flow of accurate and truthful information is essential to serving the public interest and contributing to informed decision-making in a democratic society.
- *Competition.* Promoting healthy and fair competition among professionals preserves an ethical climate, while fostering a robust business environment.
- *Disclosure of information.* Fostering open communication facilitates informed decision-making in a democratic society.
- *Safeguarding confidences.* Protecting confidential and private information, with due regard to laws and regulations regarding disclosure, protects the privacy rights of clients, organizations and individuals.
- *Conflicts of interest.* Avoiding real, potential or perceived conflicts of interest builds the trust of clients, employers and the public.
- *Enhancing the profession.* Working constantly to strengthen the public's trust in the profession builds respect and credibility for public relations.

Every PRSA member takes the following ethics pledge:

- To conduct myself professionally, with truth, accuracy, fairness and responsibility to the public;
- To improve my individual competence and advance the knowledge and proficiency of the profession through continuing research and education;
- To adhere to the articles of the Code for the practice of public relations as adopted by the governing Assembly of the Public Relations Society of America. (*PRSA Member Code of Ethics 2000*)

THE CODE OF ATHENS

The international public relations community has guidelines for ethics as well, known as the Code of Athens. It is named for the city in which it was adopted by the International Public Relations Association (IPRA) to guide professionals in more than 70 countries throughout the world.

The Code of Athens asks IPRA members to comply with the following guidelines:

- To contribute to the achievement of the moral and cultural conditions enabling human beings to reach their full stature and enjoy the indefeasible rights to which they are entitled under the Universal Declaration of Human Rights;
- To establish communication patterns and channels that, by fostering the free flow of essential information, will make each member of the society in which he lives feel that he is being informed, and also give him awareness of his own personal involvement and responsibility, and of his solidarity with other members;
- To bear in mind that, because of the relationship between his profession and the public, his conduct, even in private, will have an impact on the way in which the profession as a whole is appraised;
- To respect, in the course of his professional duties, the moral principles and rules of The Universal Declaration of Human Rights;
- To pay due regard to, and uphold, human dignity, and to recognize the right of each individual to judge for himself;
- To encourage the moral, psychological, and intellectual conditions for dialogue in its true sense, and to recognize the right of the parties involved to state their case and express their views.

A member shall undertake (the Code continues):

- To conduct himself always and in all circumstances in such a manner as to deserve and secure the confidence of those with whom he comes into contact;
- To act in all circumstances in such a manner as to take account of the respective interests of the parties involved: both the interests of the organization that he serves and the interests of the public concerned;
- To carry out his duties with integrity, avoiding language likely to lead to ambiguity or misunderstanding, and to maintain loyalty to his clients or employers, whether past or present.

A member shall refrain from:

- Subordinating the truth to other requirements;
- Circulating information that is not based on established and ascertainable facts;
- Taking part in any venture or undertaking that is unethical or dishonest or capable of impairing human dignity and integrity;
- Using any "manipulative" methods or techniques designed to create subconscious motivation that the individual cannot control of his own free will and so cannot be held accountable for the action taken on them. (*IPRA Code of Athens*)

Both the PRSA and IPRA professional codes are admirable, as is the Cadet's Code. In the final analysis, though, codes are only expressions. What matters as a person and as a professional is not what you say or recite, but rather what you do—your actions and behavior. That final thought begs for a closing quote. Try this one from Edmund Burke, Irish philosopher, statesman (1729–97): *"The only thing necessary for the triumph of evil is for good men to do nothing."*

Believe it.

INTERACTIVE EXERCISES CHAPTER 3

The Professional's Code of Conduct: A Matter of Ethics

Exercise One

Below are two scenarios. Read and identify them as to compliance with or in violation of the PRSA Member Code of Ethics 2000 or the IPRA Code of Athens:

A. A public relations practitioner, who belongs to PRSA, writes and distributes a news release to the media, but soon discovers it includes false claims about a product. Management wants to "let it ride." The boss says, "No one will notice the error." How do you respond? Would this be in compliance or violation?

B. A PRSA member sends out a news release, purporting to originate from a grassroots organization, rather than the actual client. Compliance or violation?

Exercise Two

Write your own interpretation of the limitations of the statement at the beginning of the PRSA Member Code of Ethics 2000:

"This Code applies to PRSA members. The Code is designed to be a useful guide for PRSA members as they carry out their ethical responsibilities."

Include a discussion of ethics outside the membership.

Use the CD-ROM to check your responses.

THE BASICS: THE FORMS, FORMULAS AND USES OF THE VARIOUS TYPES OF RELEASES

## CHAPTER FOUR

THE FIVE Ws AND THE FWSH: FORMULAS FOR WRITING EFFECTIVE COPY

The essential difference between writing for public relations and almost all other forms of writing is that in writing for public relations *you are trying to make something happen—or keep something from happening.*

Other forms of writing are rarely intended to move people to take an action or form an opinion. In public relations, every writing effort is concentrated on achieving a result that advances the client's or the organization's interests.

Public relations writing tries to accomplish this objective by:

- informing,
- educating,
- motivating,
- persuading and
- advocating.

For example,

- You *inform* potential customers that the client has just introduced a new product they can't be without, so they'll *do something*—they'll buy the product.
- You *educate* legislators about the negative effects a proposed piece of legislation will have on local employment—so they *don't do something*—they don't support it.
- You *persuade* local opinion leaders that the client's plans to remove the landmark old department store on Main Street and build new corporate headquarters is a positive move for the city, so they'll *let the client do something*—obtain approval for construction.
- You *motivate* employees to higher productivity, so the company becomes more competitive and jobs are more secure.
- You *advocate* major changes in the K–12 school system to improve education, so the company has a larger pool of capable employees.

TWO FUNDAMENTAL RULES AND TWO KEY FORMULAS

Good writing that is focused on clear goals helps encourage these kinds of results and is the foundation on which effective public relations programs are built. Failure to understand the desired outcome is where much public relations writing (and many public relations programs) misses the mark. So the first rule of writing for public relations is: know what you are trying to achieve. The second is: know who you need to reach. In other words, who is your audience, what do they need to know, and why do they need to know it?

There are two formulas to apply that will help you create writing that makes something happen.

One is the Five Ws and an H—that old standard of news writing.

The other is the Fwsh.

The Five Ws tell you what to put in the story and how to organize it.

The Fwsh (pronounced like "wish" with an F) is the formula that helps insure you produce copy focused on achieving a specific result. While it also stands for five Ws and an H, it specifically applies to writing for public relations.

NEWS AND THE FIVE Ws

Much of the writing done for public relations is intended for distribution by the commercial news media—newspapers, radio and television, and magazines.

There are reasons for this. Having your material distributed by the commercial media is a highly effective way to reach a large number of people rapidly and at minimum cost. More importantly, the use of your material by any of the commercial media gives it a significance and credibility not otherwise available. It suggests to the reader that an objective third party has considered the facts, found them notable and worthy, and has passed them on to the public as valid.

To be suitable for use by the commercial media, your material must qualify as *news*. It must be considered important or interesting or significant enough to be considered for the limited amount of print-space or air-time available on a daily basis. Editors or news directors must be able to serve their own objective, which is to assemble a large enough audience to attract advertisers. As a result, you must compete with others for print-space and air-time.

WHAT IS NEWS?

What is *news*? Definitions vary, but news is generally taken to mean timely *new* information about recent events or happenings that are of significance or general interest—or revelations about hitherto unknown events or happenings, the secret and the mysterious made public.

Journalists shy from definitions of news because definitions are too limiting, but they use an example to help describe the nature of the thing: "Man Bites Dog" is news; "Dog Bites Man" is not.

For the purposes of this discussion, assume that *news* is new information that is any or all of the following: important, interesting, significant, timely, hitherto unknown or unsuspected.

The material you give to the commercial media in the hope it will be used must not only qualify as news under this general definition, but it also must *look* like news—it must look and read like a news story.

Almost all news stories are hung on a skeleton whose form is as old as journalism itself. It remains the most efficient framework for getting the necessary information to the intended audience concisely and with impact.

That framework is the Five Ws and an H:

1. **Who?**
2. **What?**
3. **Where?**
4. **When?**
5. **Why?**
    And **How?**

Journalists learn to report and write their stories following this template. They never abandon it. It's too good. Public relations writers should do likewise.

THE INVERTED PYRAMID

News stories are constructed so the lead paragraph (the first paragraph of the story) contains all—or at least the most important—of the Five Ws and H, with succeeding paragraphs fleshing out the details and providing more in-depth information. The premise is: if the reader reads only the headline and the lead, he has the story. If she reads the second paragraph and beyond she will be more informed.

This approach is known as the inverted pyramid style of constructing a story. It presents the most important information first and plays out the rest in descending order of importance. There is a very practical reason behind this approach. It allows editors to fit stories to the amount of space available without risk of losing the most newsworthy information. If they run out of room, they simply cut from the bottom.

Because the inverted pyramid style is so effective, public relations writing follows this same form. It is an excellent organizing discipline, *and it looks like news.*

AN EXAMPLE OF THE FIVE Ws AT WORK

Here is an example of how the Five Ws work in two hypothetical releases.

Santa Clara, Calif., Sept. 16—A new pocket PC with advanced wireless capabilities that give users full access to Internet and cellular technology from any location will be unveiled by Everywhere, Inc., during a special meeting for distributors at San Francisco's Moscone Center today.

- Who—Everywhere, Inc.
- What—a new pocket PC with full wireless capabilities.
- When—today.
- Where—San Francisco's Moscone Center.
- Why—to enable users to make full use of mobile technology wherever they may be.

Or,

Stockton, Calif., Jan. 12—It is 75 miles inland from the sea, but early next week Stockton will begin accepting ocean-going vessels too big to transit the Panama Canal—the payoff of a $125 million expansion program designed to allow the Port of Stockton to handle new super-sized ocean-going cargo vessels and give it a competitive edge on other California ports.

- Who—The Port of Stockton.
- What—ready to accept super-sized ocean-going cargo vessels.
- Where—at the Port.
- When—early next week.
- Why—to improve the Port's competitive position.

Having written a lead that covers the Five Ws, the next step is to elaborate on these points in succeeding paragraphs.

Sometimes the lead contains only the *what* or the *why* or the *who*. Sometimes the lead is only one sentence. Sometimes it's an entire paragraph. The content of the lead and how many of the Five Ws appear within it is determined by the writer. In making that judgment, remember that the lead has two functions: (1) to provide a concise summary of the important points of the story, and (2) *equally as important, to draw the reader into the story.* In order to draw the reader into the story, you have to identify interesting or important facts and include them in the lead. Unlike a journalist, the public relations writer is not in the business of delivering information for information's sake. He is in the business of delivering information with an end result in mind—which brings us to Fwsh.

THE FWSH: THE FIVE Ws OF PUBLIC RELATIONS WRITING

The *Five Ws* provide the format for organizing the story and the formula for the information it should contain. It can apply to *any* story.

Fwsh provides the mental discipline for producing a piece of writing that is designed to achieve a specific result. It applies to *every* story.

Fwsh, as noted earlier, is short for Five Ws and an H. The acronym is intended to help you remember the steps more easily. The Fwsh is *the Five Ws of public relations writing.* Do not confuse the Fwsh with the Five Ws and H of news writing, as the styles are separate and distinct. But they can work together to help you focus your writing and get results.

The elements of the Fwsh are outlined in the six key questions below. You need to think these through carefully and be sure you understand the answers fully before you begin writing.

1. *Why am I doing this?* You want something to happen; you want a specific result as the pay-off for this effort. What is it?
2. *Whom do I need to reach?* You don't need to reach everyone. You need to reach those whose actions or opinions can help you attain your goal or those who can keep you from reaching it. It might be customers, if you are promoting a product; potential donors, if you are representing a not-for-profit organization seeking contributions, or voters, if you are trying to pass a referendum.

3. *What do they need to know?* What information do you need to provide and what ideas do you want to present, in order to motivate your audience to take the action you have identified as your objective?

4. *Where do I post my message so it is most likely to be noticed by those I am trying to reach?* Are you after major metropolitan dailies, women's magazines, radio talk shows in mid-size markets, weekly newspapers in rural counties, alumni publications?

5. *When do I make my move?* Timing is very important. Do you distribute a broad-scale release as rapidly as possible? Are you trying for early evening television news programs? Are you aiming to meet the deadlines of the business and news weekly magazines? Or are you trying to bury the story as deeply as possible?

6. *How do I package the story?* Do you work it as a news story, a feature, an op-ed piece, a video news release (VNR) for TV, a speech?

Answer these questions carefully and thoughtfully and you will be prepared to begin to write material designed to make things happen.

EXAMPLE OF HOW FWSH WORKS

Here is an example of how the Fwsh would work, and consequently guide your writing, as applied to the information in the Everywhere, Inc. lead.

- Why (the objective)? To attract attention to, and create interest in, the new wireless pocket PC—interest that can later be converted into sales.
- Who needs to know (target audience)? All potential buyers of the product, with particular emphasis on young executives, ages 24–40, in the financial services, high-tech and consulting fields.
- What do they need to know (the selling message)? This new product gives them instant access to information and key contacts wherever they are and whenever they want it.
- Where will your target audience most likely see or read the story (the distribution channels)? Business and lifestyle sections of metropolitan daily newspapers, business magazines, technology and high-tech magazines, wire services (Associated Press, United Press International, Bloomberg, Reuters), selected radio and TV news directors, and selected high-tech columnists.
- When to file the story (timing)? The best time to send a release to most outlets is 10 a.m. on Wednesday. The mid-week timing allows weekly periodicals sufficient time to work the story, yet still consider it timely enough to qualify as news. The mid-morning timing allows evening newscasts time to work the story, if they see feature possibilities. Morning dailies have all the time needed to do additional reportage or interviewing for an expanded story, if one appeals to them.
- How should it be packaged (the form)? The story will be packaged as straight news and moved by all appropriate media—wire, email, FAX, messenger.

The Five Ws and the Fwsh marry journalistic and public relations methods. They are key tools for public relations writers working to create buy-in for their client's ideas or products.

INTERACTIVE EXERCISES CHAPTER 4

The Five Ws and the Fwsh: Formulas for Writing Effective Copy

Exercise One

The release on the next page was moved by PRSA to announce winners of a national public relations campaign competition. Study the release and do the following:

A. Identify the Five Ws.
B. Write an alternate lead based on the information in the release.

(Note: for space purposes, only the first page of the release is shown, but that is all you need for the assignment.)

Exercise Two

In this exercise, we're going to practice applying the Fwsh formula. Here's the case (a real one):

> Bank of America is in a period of steadily increasing profits, but nevertheless is laying off employees, an action made necessary, it says, in order to cut costs and thereby help insure profits stay high. Among the employees losing positions are grounds maintenance workers. Since untidy grounds reflect poorly on the Bank, it has asked the still-employed personnel at its branches to "volunteer" their personal time, after-hours and on weekends, to remove litter and otherwise spruce up the grounds and parking lots—work that otherwise would have been attended to by the laid-off workers. The local newspaper learns of the situation and runs a prominently displayed story, charging that employees are being intimidated into giving up personal time to do work for which the Bank ought to be paying. The story is highly critical. You are the Bank's public relations representative. Your boss, the head of the branch banking system, calls you in and tells you the story is damaging to the Bank's relationship with its clients. He wants to get out a release that will help people see the Bank's side of the story. "Our side," he says, "is that costs are too high and that layoffs are necessary to help bring costs down, so that the Bank can stay healthy and the remaining employees can have secure jobs." More important, though, he says, "is that our people really want to help, and they are freely volunteering to do this work and are not being pressured to do so."

A. How you would apply the Fwsh formula to this particular opportunity, i.e., define the objective of the action, identify who needs to be reached, etc.? Write your answer in the space below.
B. Next, would you advise that a release be done at all, or that the Bank simply go about its business without responding to the criticism? Either way, explain in the form of a short written note to the boss.

Use the CD-ROM to compare your answers with our responses.

FOR IMMEDIATE RELEASE

CONTACT: Cedric L. Bess
212-460-1495
cedric.bess@prsa.org

PRSSA STUDENTS ROLL OUT THE RED CARPET FOR FORD MOTOR CREDIT
University of South Carolina Team Selected 2004 Bateman Competition Champions

NEW YORK (May 13, 2004) – Since nearly two thirds of today's college students will graduate with an estimated $17,000 in student loans, the importance of teaching credit education has never been more essential. Public relations students from the University of South Carolina have produced a credit education program that not only "opens doors," but also has earned them a national championship in an annual public relations campaign competition.

The Red Carpet Group from the University of South Carolina Chapter of the Public Relations Student Society of America (PRSSA) and their "Credit Opens Doors" credit education campaign won first place in the 2004 PRSSA Bateman Case Study Competition, sponsored by Ford Motor Credit Company. Creating a new and innovative approach to promote credit literacy among high school and college students was the focus of the competition. Now in its 31ˢᵗ year, the award was named in honor of the late J. Carroll Bateman, APR, past president of the Public Relations Society of America (PRSA) and one of the founding fathers of PRSSA.

"College students need real world experience in establishing a public relations campaign and this one supported our goal of educating the public about the smart use of credit," said Vice President, Public Affairs, Ford Motor Credit Company, Ron Iori. "All three of the finalists produced a high quality of work and exhibited the creative energy necessary to produce effective campaigns."

The Red Carpet Group was among three teams selected to compete in the finals of the 2004 Bateman Competition, held recently at the world headquarters of the Ford Motor Company in Dearborn, Mich. The students presented their campaigns to a panel of judges representing Ford Motor Credit and PRSA. Loyola University New Orleans placed second with their "Take Charge" campaign, while Palmetto Solutions, the second representative from the University of South Carolina in the finals, received third place for their campaign, "Your Credit, Your Future." Each team received a monetary award and will be recognized at the Society's annual awards dinner during the 2004 PRSSA National Conference, to be held in New York City in October.

- More -

## CHAPTER FIVE

WHAT MAKES A STORY?

A story is *an accounting or recital of an incident, an event, an experience, a subject, whether true or fictional, intended to interest or amuse the hearer or reader; a tale.*

We live by stories. Stories are how we explain ourselves to each other, how we convey our wants needs, fears and hopes. Stories are the way we unravel the unexplainable and make acceptable the uncertainties. Stories teach, inform, motivate and comfort. They are what shape our humanity.

One of the most important portfolios public relations carries is story-telling—telling our *story* . . . getting our *story* across . . . making sure our side of the *story* is heard. To be sure, we're talking about "stories" of the true, not fictional, variety. But it's story-telling nonetheless.

What makes a story?

Stories are made from information, ideas and images that grab and hold the interest and imagination of the audience. They speak of conflict, striving, tension and mystery, of failure and success, of surprise and marvel. They tell of good goals achieved and evil thwarted. They show us the significant and the trivial.

Whether fact or fiction, these are the parts of a story. And the story-teller uses them to grab and hold the listener's interest.

GRAB AND HOLD THEIR ATTENTION

How?

Things that are important are usually (but not always) of interest.

Things that are unusual, unexpected, mysterious, exotic, threatening or revealing can usually be counted on to spark interest and engage the imagination. Hang the opening of your story on any such hook and you will get attention.

Matters of great importance pose a larger and more difficult challenge. These subjects are often very complex, frequently boring, can cause eyes to glaze over from arcane facts and expert-speak, and require more attention and thought than most care to give, especially if we can otherwise be entertained or distracted. However, making things of importance understandable and interesting enough to be noticed and attended to is one of the most important and rewarding challenges in writing for public relations.

Here is a way to meet that challenge.

Determine the reader's (listener's, watcher's) interest and weave your story around that angle.

What is meant by "interest?" Interest is something in which the reader has a stake, that which commands her attention and influences her actions. Call it "self-interest"—the things important to her ego, her ethic, her sense of "what's-good-for-me-and-what-I-want." Never underestimate the power of the WIIFM ("What's in it for me?") mentality.

Basic emotions are foremost in this category—love, hate, fear, sorrow, joy, self-preservation—and all their offspring: money, comfort, status, ease, prestige, advantage.

THE IMPORTANCE OF SELF-INTEREST

Just as important are the reader's (or listener's or watcher's) *specific* interests—such as sports or politics or country music or cooking or Civil War history or new technology.

Fashion the story on your reader's *self-interest* and *interests* and you'll hook him or her—assuming you tell it well, which is what the craft of writing is all about.

Here are two examples of situations that require a focus on interests:

Edwards University is a fine liberal arts institution with a long history of academic and sports accomplishments. The school has decided to drop its intercollegiate football program, a decision made as a result of a combination of factors. Operating costs are high and the school's budget is tight. Compounding this is Title IX, a federal regulation that requires schools to achieve equity in men's and women's sports programs, which in essence means schools must invest as much money into women's sports as into men's sports. Football commands the largest portion of the school's sports budget. The University feels it can't afford to support football at its present level and still meet the requirements of Title IX. Therefore, Edwards decides to drop football entirely, de-emphasize highly competitive major sports overall, and re-emphasize academic excellence as the core mission of the University. Football has a special history and heritage at Edwards. The game has been a proud part of the school's history and has a strong alumni following. The elimination of the program will be big news for local sports fans and the school's powerful group of alumni supporters. It will also be fairly big news to sports followers and within the collegiate community nationally.

Assume you've been assigned to tell this story on behalf of the University and that your principal targets are students and alumni. Where does the reader's interest lie in this story? Where do the reader's and the University's interests intersect? Many people are going to be unhappy with this decision—local restaurants and motels who count on game day business, the vendors who work the stands, Edwards football fans on campus and around the country, among others. Some will applaud vigorously—those who think an emphasis on sports detracts from the University's mission, certain members of the faculty who disapprove of highly competitive intercollegiate sports in general, supporters of Title IX. The University will lose ticket revenue and perhaps even monetary support from sports-oriented alumni.

How do you present this story?

Or assume you've been assigned to write the story introducing the formation of the new charitable foundation being underwritten by Gordon Moore, the co-founder of Intel. To be called the Gordon and Betty Moore Foundation, its initial funding will make it one of the largest philanthropic ventures in the country. The Foundation will focus exclusively on higher education in the sciences at the graduate level, on medical research, and on the relatively ambiguous environmental concept of "bio-diversity," by which is meant protecting "the gene pool of the planet." The Foundation will focus its funding on programs that can be expected to produce unusually good results in relatively short time frames, if suitably large amounts of money are applied. It will accept more risk than foundations normally find comfortable, but it expects higher returns. Who is the target audience and what will interest them?

Your job is to hook and hold the audience and get the client's key points across. Which storylines do you choose?

INTERACTIVE EXERCISES CHAPTER 5

What Makes a Story?

Exercise One

We're going to use the two story example laid out in this chapter to practice how we choose and present the facts available to best make our client's case.

A. First, the "Edwards University Drops Football" story. Assume you represent Edwards University and your objective is to put this decision in the most positive light for the majority of your constituents. What storyline do you follow? Why is that your choice? Write the lead.

B. Now assume you represent the Moore Foundation. The obvious storylines are "High Tech Billionaire Establishes Results-Oriented Foundation" and "Biodiversity to Be Focus of New Multi-billion Dollar Trust." What storyline do you take? Is one necessarily better than the other? Is there another storyline you find more compelling?

Exercise Two

Do the Fwsh for the Moore Foundation story.

Use the CD-ROM to compare your answers with our suggestions.

## CHAPTER SIX

GETTING THE INFORMATION YOU NEED

The odds of someone handing you a neatly wrapped package containing all the information you need to write a release are very low. You will need to ferret out the details yourself. In the news world, this process is called reporting. In business and academia, it is called research. In all three arenas, it is a serious exercise and hard work.

Consider, again, the Everywhere, Inc. story.

If you were working for the agency that serves Everywhere, Inc., the account executive would probably call you in and say, "Everywhere, Inc. is ready to launch an important new product that has exciting possibilities and real benefits for users. Give me a release that will draw attention and help support the marketing drive." If you are a member of the Everywhere, Inc. public relations team, your boss, the public relations director, might give you essentially the same directive. Or, regardless of whether you work for the agency or the company, you may very well come up with the idea yourself. Knowing what should be highlighted to help a client reach its goals, when to do this and how to do it, is an important part of the public relations job.

So how do you get the information you need to construct the story so it appeals to your target audience and evokes the desired response?

GO TO THE SOURCE

Get it from the people who have it. In the case of Everywhere, Inc., you'll likely need to meet with the product manager, the technical team, and the marketing people. Work through the Fwsh and Five Ws with them until you find out:

- what this thing is and what it does
- why it's important
- how this product differs from others on the market
- when and where it will be available
- what it will cost.

You'll need good quotes from the technical people on why the product is superior to its competition. If they do not have good quotes ready, you help them phrase some. If the product was test-marketed, find out if any of the reactions of early users are worth including (for example, "I found this gives me more flexibility than any product I've used," said John Public, a sales executive for a sports marketing firm and a member of the test market group).

In short, act like a good reporter. Ask many questions. Cover the story. When you know everything that might be interesting or important about the product, you are ready to start writing.

Keep in mind, however, just understanding the subject isn't enough.

SO WHAT?

One more question must be answered, if you are to craft a story designed to advance a goal. The million-dollar question is: "So what?" or "Who cares?" You must never start your story without knowing the answer.

Regardless of how simplistic the subject, the writer must be able to make it special, important or different enough to grab and hold the attention and interest of the targeted audience.

Why should anyone care about the product? If you can demonstrate why this particular new product can be important to your audience or make their work easier or more efficient, or how it ties into their other interests, they will care. This is called the "benefits proposition." Show the benefits, whether of a product, a service, an idea or an action, that tie into the readers' interests, and they will care. Everywhere, Inc.'s "so what?" is that people can have instant access to the Internet and make contact through their cellular devices, regardless of their location. The "who cares?" covers everyone for whom the ability to be in contact is important.

The ability to identify the "so what?" and "who cares?" is a function of imagination and curiosity. Keep working until your interest is piqued, until you understand what can, should or will be important to the audience. Use imagination and creativity to capture those ideas and concepts, to shape and refine them using compelling words and imagery. If you are successful in doing so, you won't have a problem with "So what?" or "Who cares?"

To recap, find the information you need by going after it. You do the reporting: set up interviews, research the facts, test ideas, ask *all* the questions. Know what is right and good and exciting about your subject, but also be fully aware of what can be criticized. *All* the questions, particularly those that reveal potential problems with the product, must be asked. If all the questions aren't asked, all the answers can't be covered.

Occasionally clients or employers will want stories about things that are so arcane and esoteric or so unimportant and insignificant, that it is unlikely anything can be made of them. Still, the professional's job is to make the arcane and the esoteric understandable and interesting, if at all possible. This can present a fairly exciting creative challenge. On rare occasions, careful thought and consideration may reveal something significant or interesting. But, if in the end there is no story, the writer's job is to say so. The insignificant and unimportant must be identified for what they are. That old saw about sow's ears and silk purses is true.

INTERACTIVE EXERCISES CHAPTER 6

Getting the Information You Need

Exercise One

Read the following release and identify the "So what?" and "Who cares?" elements in the story.

KAISER PERMANENTE.

FOR IMMEDIATE RELEASE

Northern California News Bureau
Maureen McInaney
(510)987-4779
(510)987-3900

KAISER PERMANENTE RESEARCHERS WILL EVALUATE EFFECT OF LIFESTLYE CHANGES ON WOMEN WITH BREAST CANCER

OAKLAND, Calif., November 8, 2004 Researchers at Kaiser Permanente have received a $10 million grant to study whether lifestyle factors such as diet, exercise and use of complementary and alternative medicine (CAM) impact recurrence and survival rates for women with breast cancer.

"When a woman is diagnosed with breast cancer, she wants to know what she can do to deal with the disease," said Lawrence Kushi, ScD, associate director for etiology and prevention at Kaiser Permanente of Northern California (KPNC) and lead investigator. "She has many questions. Should she change her diet, take supplements, eat soy?

"She may get advice from many places, but there is surprisingly little data to guide her," he said. "This study, the largest of its kind, will provide some of the first scientific evidence to address these issues."

While there are many studies that have examined the association of dietary and other factors with risk of getting breast cancer, few studies have examined whether diet, exercise and the use of CAM therapies improve prognosis for women with the disease, he explained. Some of the only other studies to address these questions are being conducted by other KPNC researchers, and this study will build upon that knowledge, said Kushi.

How these factors influence prognosis may depend, in part, on molecular characteristics that influence how DNA is damaged or repaired, he said, adding that it may also be true that DNA anomalies impact how genes express themselves. He explained that these markers may influence outcomes for women or interact with conventional therapies such as chemotherapy and radiation.

Exercise Two

A. Who are the primary targets for the release? (List your targets here.)

_____

_____

_____

_____

B. Are there secondary targets for this release? (List your secondary targets here.)

_____

_____

_____

_____

C. What contacts did the writer use to gather information necessary for writing this story? (List them here.)

_____

_____

_____

_____

Use the CD-ROM to compare your answers with our responses.

## CHAPTER SEVEN

THE FIVE TYPES OF RELEASES AND HOW TO WRITE FOUR OF THEM

A "release" is information cast in news story form that is intended to be made public through the print and broadcast media. Releases are the traditional way in which companies and organizations get their news and information to mass audiences.

There are five basic types of releases. The public relations writer needs to master at least four of them. The fifth type, the financial release, is a specialty that requires an understanding of the financial reporting rules that govern companies whose stock is publicly traded. This type of release is best left to senior writers who are qualified to work with such information.

The four types of releases the public relations practitioner is expected to handle are:

1. Hard News
2. News-Feature
3. Product or Service (in support of the marketing operation)
4. Personnel

Both product and personnel releases can qualify as hard news if the information they carry is of enough importance, but usually news in these categories is handled in the ways described below.

HARD NEWS RELEASES

"Hard news" has two components:

1. The subject involves something substantive that has happened or is about to happen, or it contains new information about an issue or an action of consequence.
2. The matter is time-sensitive and should be communicated as rapidly as possible, due to its importance, uniqueness or immediacy.

Announcing that company X plans to merge with company Y, or that X plans to lay-off a sizeable number of employees, constitutes hard news. An announcement that X has scored a major technological breakthrough, or has just selected a new CEO, or is making a large monetary commitment to provide daycare for the children of employees is "hard" news in that important matters are involved.

A company's expansion plans, changes in management at the senior executive level, mergers or acquisitions, plant or office openings or closures, or any development that can, or should be, considered important to an organization's constituents or the public in general is hard news. Without exception, hard news should be released as quickly as possible and to as broad an audience as appropriate. Be careful not to sacrifice accuracy in your desire to move hard news quickly, however.

NEWS-FEATURE RELEASES

News-features and general features have less immediate news value. They aren't as time sensitive. They can play tomorrow or next week. While time isn't a major factor, timing often is. Feature stories are created by the way the writer is able to make a matter interesting or entertaining. The stories often turn on the unusual, the unique, the unexpected or the unlikely. They are intended to appeal to the reader's interests and curiosity. A hard news story draws attention through the importance of what is being reported. News-features draw attention through the skillful presentation of the material. The writer isn't limited to the inverted pyramid form and has the flexibility to employ some of the techniques of fiction writers, such as mood setting, word picture descriptions, dialogue, indirect quotes, etc., in shaping her piece. (Check out some of the writing in *The Literary Journalists* referred to in the Suggested Readings in the Et Cetera section at the back of the book.)

News-features take advantage of the attention generated by a hard news release or a recent action or event by adding a human interest element to the story. This is precisely why the timing of the news-feature can be so important. Timing isn't much of a consideration for general features. These are stories that cover matters of broader interest. For example, they might focus on subjects such as new developments in old technology that are making a difference for users today, or explore how new security requirements are causing businesses to change they way suppliers and customers are treated. There is nothing particularly time sensitive in the subjects that general features address.

PRODUCT AND MARKETING RELEASES

Everyone is selling something—products or services, hopes or ideas. That's how people stay in business and institutions stay viable. Writing that sells is the bread-and-butter of those working in public relations. The purest representation of that form is a marketing release. These releases, which are often called product releases or product publicity, represent the largest and most cost-efficient output of most public relations operations. This is true whether that operation is serving business and industry, not-for-profits or governments.

Marketing releases are designed to attract attention to, and create interest in, a product or service in direct support of the marketing effort. These pieces hinge on benefits. They show the reader the important things the product or service can do for them—the *benefit* that will come as a result of owning the product or using the service. This is intended to motivate the reader to seek out the product, or at least more information. Product releases may qualify as either hard news or news-feature, depending on the significance of the product. In either case, the product or the service must be accurately represented. Overstatement or puffery (phrases like "outstanding," or "best of its type," or "unequalled") are immediate flags to editors that the story is an attempt at disguising advertising as legitimate news, or that it's merely a piece of fluff without news value. If a story is seen as such, the only place it will make a showing is in the trash can.

PERSONNEL RELEASES

Personnel releases are used to highlight the quality and competence of your client's management and personnel. They announce the new talent being brought into the organization or the promotion of employees already on staff to positions of increased responsibility or authority. These releases serve a variety of purposes. They let customers and shareholders, as well as employees and competitors, know the caliber of people working for the organization and the skills and strengths being added to company operations. They provide a quick and important introduction, through the media, for the new hire and help establish credibility for him or her within the organization. They underscore the strengths and competitiveness of the organization by showing that its performance is solid enough to attract such talent.

The format for personnel releases is usually simple and routine: a short opening paragraph announcing who has been hired or promoted and what position he or she will fill. This is followed by a paragraph describing the job responsibilities, with emphasis on the strengths and experience the individual brings to the position. A short quote from the appropriate senior official follows, along with a recitation of the person's credentials, and a brief quote from the new hire to close the release. The writing is straightforward and concise, and effusive comments about the individual are to be avoided.

Personnel releases are important. They showcase what most organizations believe to be their most important asset—their employees.

FINANCIAL RELEASES

Financial releases are reports on the strengths, achievements and condition of publicly traded companies (companies whose stock is available to the general public and is traded on one of the major stock exchanges, such as the New York Stock Exchange). This highly specialized writing is a task journeymen writers are unlikely to be assigned. It requires a solid background in financial reporting and an understanding of the regulatory issues and rules concerning what publicly traded companies may, and must, communicate to shareholders and the public. Even so, beginners should at least understand what it covers, and when and why it is used.

The most common forms of financial releases are quarterly and annual earnings and dividend releases, and announcements concerning funding, credit ratings, etc. Financial releases are always handled as hard news.

Financial writing involves far more than releases. A large, and perhaps more important part of the responsibility includes preparation of the company's annual report, presentations for security analysts meetings, speeches to financial and economic groups, special communications to shareholders, and, on occasion, white papers on matters of economic or financial policy.

EXAMPLES

The easiest way to understand how to construct each of the releases covered is to study good examples. Some quality examples of the four basic forms follow. Study these carefully and use them as a template for your writing.

Hard News

The release below shows the standard format for a news release. Remember that news releases carry information about an event, action or happening, that is of importance and/or interest to its intended audience. It represents a significant development and is new information. Finally, it is about to occur, is occurring now, or has just occurred.

In this case the "news" is of importance and interest to anyone who may need nursing services now or in the future, or who has friends or family who may (which is almost everyone at some point). It also targets people who aspire to careers in nursing, and hospital and health care professionals charged with providing these services.

The action is significant, because it addresses a critical need and has a level of funding likely to lead to its success.

Note that the Five Ws are all covered in the first paragraph. Also take note of the lack of puffery. The story is told simply in straightforward terms.

As for distribution, the story moved simultaneously to print and broadcast media via BusinessWire. It was also e-mailed or faxed to a list of key writers, editors and columnists (by name), who could be expected to have an interest in the story by virtue of their beats or stories they had written previously, and was delivered by e-mail and fax to other selected contacts as appropriate. Finally, it was posted on the Foundation's web site and the employee e-mail bulletin board.

Notice the structure. This format, or one similar, is typical of the style used by most organizations.

New Initiative Aimed At Crisis In Nursing   *(A)*

FOR IMMEDIATE RELEASE   *(B)*

CONTACT: Genny Biggs   *(C)*
Gordon and Betty Moore Foundation
Phone: 415-561-7722

(D)

San Francisco, November 19—The Board of the Gordon and Betty Moore Foundation announced today the approval of a 10-year, $110 million Betty Irene Moore Nursing Initiative to improve the quality of nursing-related patient care in five counties of the San Francisco Bay Area. The effort will be focused in Alameda, Marin, San Francisco, San Mateo and Santa Clara counties.

The Foundation will address the crisis in nursing care by funding projects to increase the quantity of registered nurses (RNs) in the San Francisco Bay Area and improve clinical skills effectiveness. "Quality of care for hospital patients is threatened as the shortage of nurses progressively worsens," said Betty Moore, co-founder and member of the Board of Directors. "If left unaddressed, these issues will become a severe public health problem."

"We hope to have a substantial and lasting impact on nursing-related patient care in acute care hospitals, as measured by improved patient outcomes," said Ed Penhoet, chief program officer for Science and Higher Education.

The Foundation will fund projects to increase the number of experienced, qualified RNs and expand the number of available training programs in the Bay Area. According to the American Hospital Association, nurses represent the largest healthcare workforce and provide approximately 95 percent of patient care in the hospitals, but the United States currently faces a nursing shortage of more than 126,000 RNs. The Bureau of Labor Statistics projects a shortfall of approximately one million RNs by 2010. The field of nursing has been challenged by the rapid pace of developments in medical technology. The shortened patient stays, greater disease complexity, and more acute illness in the aging patient population compound this situation.

The portfolio of grants that constitutes the Betty Irene Moore Nursing Initiative is designed to have a synergistic impact on improving nursing care by addressing both the shortage of nurses and the need for more RN training in medical technology and treatment. In keeping with the Foundation's emphasis on the measurability of its grantmaking effectiveness, staff will compare changes in patient outcomes related to nursing care such as adverse events, complications, and patient and family satisfaction.

(E)

About the Foundation
The Gordon and Betty Moore Foundation was established in November 2000, by Intel cofounder Gordon Moore and his wife Betty. The Foundation funds outcome-based projects that will measurably improve the quality of life for future generations. Grantmaking is concentrated in initiatives that support the Foundation's principal areas of concern regarding the environment, higher education, scientific research, and the San Francisco Bay Area. (F)

Template Explanation
A. A headline summarizes the story, so news media can get a fast fix on the subject of the piece.
B. This line sets the time at which the release may be made public. "FOR IMMEDIATE RELEASE" means the news outlet can use it as soon as it is received. Releases are sometimes given to news outlets to be held for release at a later time, as in "For Release no earlier than 10:30 a.m., Tuesday, May 8," or "HOLD FOR RELEASE: April 10." This is called putting an "embargo" on the release. Embargoing is a risky practice. Don't trust competitive media outlets to hold news. If you're ready to put it out, be ready for it to be used.
C. This line identifies the person the media should contact to obtain additional information or to answer questions.
D. Then the story itself runs.
E. A symbol such as a series of #s or "30" (an old wire-service sign-off signal) indicates the end of the story. Multi-page releases carry a "more" or "more to come" line at the end of each page when more copy follows.
F. The "boiler plate" paragraph—a summary of facts about the organization, provides basic background information.

A Feature Release

Here is an example of a feature release. It contains no hard news. The story is built, instead, on human interest. In this case, the focus is on a welfare mother overcoming adversity to care for her two young sons and ailing mother. While the story is about the mother's achievement, it also highlights the client's loan programs for small businesses. Essentially, it's a subtle promotion for the services and products the bank offers. Feature releases always spin off leads designed to draw the reader into the piece based on its appeal as story of interest—not its importance per se.

Margolin
Associates
FOR IMMEDIATE RELEASE
CONTACT: LISA MARGOLIN-FEHER
            (858) 350-1551
            Email: lisa@margohnpr.com

BUSINESS IN THE BARRIO:
For SBA Award Winner, Arduous Journey
From Welfare to "Work is Child's Play"

San Diego, Calif., April 28—Just eight years ago, Gale Walker spent her days trying to make ends meet. A single mother of two, she reluctantly turned to welfare after forfeiting a job to take care of her ailing mother.

When welfare wasn't enough, and with limited resources, Walker started a home day-care business to be able to earn a little income and still be at home with her kids. Today, Walker, winner of this year's U. S. Small Business Administration Welfare-to-Work Entrepreneur of the Year award, owns Children of the Rainbow, a thriving home day-care center in San Diego's inner-city neighborhood of Logan Heights.

Walker has recently expanded her business with the help of the local offices of Bank of America, the SBA and the Small Business Development and International Trade Center. Just this month. Children of the Rainbow added a 7,000-square-foot childcare center at 3078 L St. It's open from 5 a.m. to 1 a.m.—hours that make it easier for working parents.

"I wouldn't have been able to get this far had it not been for the assistance of these partners," Walker said. Bank of America, the largest SBA lender in the United States, provided a $200,000 SBA loan to facilitate the expansion.

Children of the Rainbow's expanded facility is the only licensed child-care center for infants and toddlers in the Logan Heights/Grant Hill area. The center is critical, since federal law requires parents of infants older than 12 weeks to immediately seek work if they are receiving public assistance.

"We designed our new facility to embrace welfare-to-work and to free parents up to find jobs," Sawyer said.

#

A Product/Marketing Support Release

Product or marketing support releases are intended help create awareness of and interest in new products or services. They provide direct support for the marketing effort. Product releases focus on the same sort of values statements that advertising would cover, highlighting the benefits to the buyer. Note how quotes are used to help carry the selling message. Product and marketing support releases usually (but not always, as the second example will demonstrate) have an element of "news" in that a "new" product or service is being introduced. Product releases are often the first salvo in a marketing campaign, with the initial publicity effort followed by a comprehensive advertising program. Sometimes, publicity carries the entire program, with no direct advertising planned or needed. Here are two examples. The first is a relative straightforward release promoting "the HDTV home theatre experience." It has certain time urgency to it, since it is pegged to an upcoming news event—The Super Bowl. The second is an "evergreen," a story that can play at anytime, since it promotes the product in a generic way. This particular story is a minor masterpiece of aligning reader interest with product attributes.

For Immediate Release

Super Bowl Fever Likely to Ignite Home Theater Passion

MINNEAPOLIS, Jan. 25, 2005 – Super Bowl's status as the nation's premier "unofficial" holiday, combined with price declines in high-definition television (HDTV), are likely to accelerate consumer interest in the home theater experience, according to the professionals at Best Buy, the nation's leading consumer electronics retailer.

"Super Bowl has enjoyed a remarkable ratings run, posting an audience of close to 90 million viewers last year alone," said Lee Simonson, business team leader at Best Buy. "People tend to view the 'big game' and other nationally televised events such as the Academy Awards as social occasions. This definitely creates renewed interest in HDTV and home theater as we approach air time."

A study conducted after last year's game by global research company ASI confirms that Super Bowl is a TV-centered, social magnet. According to ASI, the "big game" not only attracts people who don't normally watch professional football game broadcasts, but it has become a party lure, twice as likely to be viewed from someone else's home with six or more people as compared to other games during the pro ball season.

It's this drawing power that could help accelerate the industry's robust 2004 sales of 7.3 million HDTV units into 2005's "big game" telecast and beyond. Compared to traditional analog television, HDTV improves the viewing experience with finer picture quality and detail, and wider display. Home theater systems further enhance the experience by adding sound. HDTV now represents the majority of industry, and Best Buy's own, television sales.

"HDTV is becoming the centerpiece of an in-home viewing experience that enables us to feel the excitement of actually being at the 'big game,'" Simonson observed. "Better yet, these theater systems can be enjoyed for a fraction of the $10,000 or more for four tickets to Jacksonville."

(more)

Super Bowl Fever Ignites HDTV Passion
Jan. 25, 2005/Page 2

Best Buy sells a wide variety of HDTVs and home theater components to help customers satisfy their viewing and listening preferences. Simonson encourages people who are contemplating a home theater system to consider all the elements that create the ideal "big game" viewing experience at home:

- **Preferred HDTV format.** HDTV is available in a wide variety of television formats. Most feature large screens in widescreen proportions simulating a theater experience at home. Plasma and LCD televisions are generating a lot of interest because they are thinner, lighter and brighter than traditional analog TVs. Other options that provide great viewing include microdisplay rear-projection televisions such as digital light processing (DLP) sets.

- **Source for digital broadcast content.** Three sources – over-the-air from local TV stations, satellite and digital cable – deliver local and national digital programming in-home, and these options can vary by market. Some high-definition televisions have a built-in tuner to receive local high-definition broadcasts. These sets are referred to as "HD-Built-In." Sets without an integrated tuner are "HD-Ready," and need a set-top box to decode the high-definition signal.

- **Sound quality.** The HDTV format incorporates digital 5.1 surround sound into high-definition broadcasts, giving the "in the middle of the action" feel. For the ultimate viewing experience, it's important to incorporate a sound system that is comparable in quality to the television. The ideal is a dedicated audio system of at least five speakers, plus a subwoofer for extreme low frequencies, and sufficient power to drive them all.

- **Assembly requirements.** It is important to have the right cables and accessories to connect the home theater system to the in-home power supply. Best Buy in-store customer specialists are available to provide advice on specific home theater cable and other set-up accessory requirements. For those customers who are hesitant about assembling the system themselves, Best Buy service personnel are available for in-home delivery and set-up, ensuring that everything is connected and calibrated for the optimal experience.

For more details about HDTV and home theater systems, visit www.bestbuynewscenter.com.

About Best Buy Co., Inc.
Best Buy Co., Inc. (NYSE: BBY) is an innovative Fortune 100® growth company that continually strives to create superior customer experiences. Through more than 780 retail stores across the United States and in Canada, our employees connect customers with technology and entertainment products and services that make life easier and more fun. We sell consumer electronics, home-office products, entertainment software, appliances and related services. A Minneapolis-based company, our operations include: Best Buy (BestBuy.com), Future Shop (FutureShop.ca), Geek Squad (GeekSquad.com) and Magnolia Audio Video (Magnoliaav.com). We support our communities through employee volunteerism and grants from The Best Buy Children's Foundation.

###

Prepared by: Dreyer's Grand Ice Cream, Inc.
                   5929 College Avenue
                   Oakland, CA 94618

Contact: Kim Goeller-Johnson (510) 601-4211   *kagoelle@dreyers.com*

MAN WITH MILLION DOLLAR 'BUDS' HAS TASTY JOB
Ice Cream Taster Has Work Licked

If you think that getting paid to eat ice cream every day is too good to be true, you haven't met **John Harrison** and his talented taste buds!

As the "Official Taster" for Dreyer's Grand Ice Cream, John has dipped his golden spoon into more than 200 million gallons of America's favorite frozen treat during his sweet career. In fact, John's taste buds are such a cool asset that they are insured for **One Million Dollars** and provide the final word on what new flavors ice cream lovers scoop up in the freezer aisle each year.

John's job isn't always *Peaches 'N Cream*...some days it's *Rocky Road* or *Butter Pecan*. But John's mission remains the same...to make sure Dreyer's ice cream meets the highest quality standard before it tops waffle cones, builds sweet foundations in sundae dishes or plays center stage in banana splits.

Born into an ice cream-making family, John learned the business as a half-pint. His family has dipped into this sweet treat for four generations...from his great-grandfather's chain of ice cream parlors in turn of the century New York City to his father's ice cream ingredients factory in Atlanta. John's ice cream roots are so firmly planted that he claims, "My blood runs 16 percent butterfat."

His subsequent 35+ years have been spent in the ice cream industry, (not eating--but tasting!) and John and his discriminating taste buds have become quite famous. In 1997, he received the Master Taster of the Year award from the American Tasting Institute.

-more-

Million Dollar Taste Buds/Page 2

At 63 years of age, John's taste buds are still in their prime. The tongue is comprised of 9,000 taste buds; each bud has ten to 15 receptacles that send messages to the brain to let you know whether you are eating something bitter, sweet, salty or sour. When sampling ice cream, the main focus of the taste buds is to decipher the quality top notes and balance of the fresh cream, sweeteners and natural flavors.

According to John, one simple thing anyone can do to enhance the ice cream eating experience is to eat ice cream at the right temperature, 10 degrees. Most people eat it right out of the freezer at about 5 degrees, but allowing ice cream to soften and warm up a little brings out the flavor.

In order to distinguish the subtleties of ice cream, John protects his taste buds. He stays away from spicy and hot foods during the week, he doesn't drink alcohol or smoke, and he drinks herbal tea to get his taste buds going in the morning.

John claims he has the best job in the world, "It's like being Willy Wonka!" However, there are some drawbacks to the job. Similar to wine tasting, John rarely swallows the ice cream -- he takes a cool spoonful, swirls it around his mouth, covering all taste buds, smacks his lips to aerate the product, brings the aroma back through his nose then unceremoniously spits it out.

In addition to his million dollar tongue, John also has a flair for developing new flavors and has been a major influence in the creation of popular favorites such as Cookies 'N Cream, New York Blueberry Cheesecake, Peanut Butter Cup, Peaches 'N Cream and Malt Ball 'N Fudge.

# # #

A Personnel Release

This is a good example of a standard personnel release. The credentials of the newly appointed executive are highlighted and the scope of his new job responsibilities delineated.

1000 Broadway, Suite 450
Oakland, CA 94607
Phone: 510.891.9400
Facsimile: 510.891.9446
www.afevans.com

For Information: May 6, 2004
Roberta Wong
Wong & Murray
925-932-6050
wmipr@aol.com
Roberta Clark
A.F. Evans Co.
510-267-4611
RobertaC@afevans.com

A.F. EVANS CO. NAMES ALAN F. GREENWALD COO
Real Estate Lawyer, Fannie Mae Multifamily Financing Expert

A.F. Evans Company, Inc., today announced that Alan F. Greenwald has joined the company as Chief Operating Officer. In this capacity, he will oversee long-term debt and equity relationships for the Company as well as assist CEO Arthur Evans with the implementation of development and management strategies.

"A.F. Evans Company has an impressive track record and solid reputation for providing housing that strengthens communities," said Mr. Greenwald. " I look forward to expanding the company's role in creating vibrant housing in markets where the need is great, such as in the Bay Area."

Prior to assuming his new position with A.F. Evans Company, Mr. Greenwald spent ten years with Fannie Mae in Washington, DC, most recently as Director, Multifamily Group. He directed efforts to arrange financing for large, multifamily property owners and was responsible for client relations with large institutional borrowers.

Previously, Mr. Greenwald was a real estate attorney for Brobeck, Phleger & Harrison, a prominent San Francisco law firm, which is no longer in practice. He has also worked at the U.S. Department of Housing and Urban Development in the Office of the Secretary and the Office of the General Counsel. A member of the State Bar of California, Mr. Greenwald has a Juris Doctor degree and a Masters degree in City and Regional Planning from the University of California, Berkeley. He is married to Lynne Grove Greenwald, a psychotherapist who is a native of Walnut Creek. They have two daughters.

Established in 1977, Oakland-based A.F. Evans Company develops and manages a diversity of projects, ranging from affordable housing, assisted living facilities to market rate apartments and condominiums. The company has completed more than 7,600 residential units in California, Nevada and Washington.

#

AF EVANS COMPANY, INC. | AF EVANS DEVELOPMENT, INC. | EVANS PROPERTY MANAGEMENT, IN

INTERACTIVE EXERCISES CHAPTER 7

The Five Types of Releases and How to Write Four of Them

Exercise One

You work for the Outerbanks University Department of Public Information. Write the lead and follow-on paragraph for a news story announcing that 18 students from Outerbanks are preparing to leave on a mission to provide aid to tsunami victims in Indonesia. The group, all upper division students in the University's College of Arts and Sciences, will work on rebuilding an aqueduct from a local fresh water lake that serves two villages on East Timor. The aqueduct was destroyed in the tsunami and the villages have been without safe drinking water for some time. The students will work under the direction of a team of construction engineers from the University's College of Engineering, who have been on site for the past two weeks. The students have no formal engineering experience, but all have worked at summer jobs in construction. The students are volunteering their time and will pay their own transportation and living costs. Construction costs will be underwritten by a grant from International Relief Agency of Zurich, Switzerland. The group is scheduled to depart from the Johnstown Airport early tomorrow morning. Outerbanks is located in Johnstown, North Carolina.

Exercise Two

You represent Dreyer's Grand Ice Cream. Write the first two paragraphs of a personnel release announcing the appointment of John Harrison to the position of Official Taster for Dreyer's Grand Ice Cream, using information from the product release in this chapter.

Exercise Three

Your agency represents a start-up named Northgate Technology. Northgate is ready to offer a new Internet service that remembers birthdays, anniversaries, and special days such as Mother's Day and Valentine's Day and automatically sends personalized cards to the special people in the clients' lives. The service also will help the clients buy appropriate gifts on-line and arrange to have the gift delivered with a note or card. The service is aimed at busy and/or forgetful people in the 25 to 60 age group and will be available at monthly charge of $9.95 plus the cost of the cards or gifts. The service is called "Always Thoughtful." Write the lead paragraph and a follow-on paragraph for a product release announcing this service.

Use the CD-ROM to check your work.

## CHAPTER EIGHT

A STEP-BY-STEP TEMPLATE FOR CONSTRUCTING A RELEASE, FROM THE LEAD TO CLEARANCES AND DISTRIBUTION

Now that you have learned about the basic forms, let's review the construction of a release step-by-step using the Fwsh and the Five Ws. This is a basic format and can be used as a template for any release at any time.

First, collect the facts on which the story will be built.

THE FACTS

Gordon Moore, the co-founder of Intel, and his wife Betty, are establishing a new philanthropic foundation out of their personal fortune. Moore will fund the venture by contributing to it some of his personal stock—enough to put it in the multi-billion-dollar range and make it one of the ten largest philanthropic foundations in the country. Moore wants the Foundation to focus on collegiate level education, scientific research and the environment.

He intends for the Foundation to use a relatively unorthodox approach to grant-making. It will take the initiative and seek out projects to support, rather than waiting for proposals to be made to it and will look for opportunities that may be a bit riskier than those funded by more conventional sources, such as government entities, but which offer the possibilities of higher returns in a shorter time span. He wants to support projects that can make a substantial contribution to the quality of life and health of the planet.

Lewis W. Coleman, a respected and experienced international financial executive, will head the new Foundation. Though he has no experience as a foundation executive, Coleman has a reputation as a creative thinker with a record of personal involvement in environmental and educational matters. He has over 30 years experience as chairman of a major international securities and investment banking company and as a vice chairman of two major international banks. He holds a degree in economics from Stanford and serves on various corporate boards, as well as on the boards of a number of not-for-profit organizations, such as Trout Unlimited.

Coleman expects the first year of operations to be devoted largely to start-up activities, such as assembling a staff and getting it organized, deciding on grant criteria and making the Foundation's agenda known.

Moore was waiting to find the right person to build and run the Foundation, before proceeding with its formation. Coleman is that man, Moore says. Coleman sees a remarkable opportunity and challenge in building the Foundation and is very excited about its potential.

Those are the facts.

THE FWSH

What is the Fwsh for this announcement?

Assuming the Foundation is the client, these are the most likely answers the Fwsh exercise would reveal.

What Do You Want to Achieve with This Release? *(Objective)*

The initial release should be to gain wide visibility for the Foundation, introducing it as an important new participant in the foundation world. It should highlight its innovative agenda and approach to finding and developing opportunities that can benefit society.

Whom Do You Need to Reach? *(Targets)*

Clearly you want to reach all those individuals and organizations working in the fields of higher education, scientific research and the environment, as they may have projects or ideas that can advance the Foundation's goal of "making a substantial contribution to the quality of life and the health of the planet." While these are the primary targets, you'll also need to consider secondary audiences, such as: other foundations, governmental research agencies and various government commissions and committees, leading academics in the Foundation's fields of concentration, potential employees, business and industry leaders and finally, the general public, to whom the benefits of all this money and activity will finally accrue.

What Do They Need to Know? *(Messages)*

They need to know the new organization is seeking to support projects that can make a substantial difference in the quality of life and the health of the planet, is willing to take risks to help make valuable things happen, and has the resources to achieve major breakthroughs.

Where Do You Post the Story to Get the Attention You Want? *(Distribution)*

The story will be filed to all key national and international print and broadcast news media, with particular emphasis on business, technology, education, scientific research, and environmental writers and commentators. Commercial wire services (Business Wire, PR Newswire and others) will be used to move the story rapidly. Simultaneously with release to the commercial wire services, the story will be moved to key writers and commentators by e-mail, FAX and with direct delivery as appropriate. Then it will be cross filed to the key media in each specific area of interest (higher education, scientific research, the environment) and to the foundation "trades"—the publications, newsletters, Web services and e-zines read by foundation professionals. In addition, messenger copies of the release with a "we thought you might be interested" note will go to the members of the various U.S. House and Senate committees involved with education, scientific research and the environment, and to the heads of the government agencies involved in these fields. A similar file will be made to selected academics at major universities and to the directors of major research institutions. Finally, the release will be posted on the Foundation's Web site.

*Wh*en Do You Make Your Move? *(Timing)*

The announcement will be made at the time of day most likely to ensure good print and broadcast media play. That means it must be sent early enough that newspapers have time to work the story fully, yet not so early as to make the story old news for drive-time radio and early evening telecasts. Good play in magazines and periodicals is also desired, so the story will move late enough in the week that it still has news value for those outlets. All things considered, an 11:45 a.m. release on Wednesday seems the right choice.

*Ho*w Will You Package the Story *(Form)*?

The announcement will be packaged as a straight news release, relying on the multi-billion-dollar size of the Foundation, its unique and aggressive approach, its "improve things for all of us" objective, and the name recognition and reputation of Dr. Moore. That's the Fwsh.

THE FIVE Ws

The Five Ws and H are:

- What—a new multi-billion-dollar charitable foundation
- Who—Gordon Moore, Intel Co-Founder and respected international business leader
- Why—to make possible projects that have the potential to significantly improve the quality of life for people everywhere and contribute to the health of the planet
- When—being organized now and will begin operations early next year
- Where—headquartered in San Francisco, but operating worldwide
- How—remember that "how" is included if it's important to the story, which it is in this case. The "How" is by finding and funding projects that can have significant results.

WRITING THE STORY STEP-BY-STEP

With the Fwsh and the Five Ws completed and the inverted pyramid style in mind, it's time to put it all together.

The Lead

The lead carries the Five Ws.

> **San Francisco, Nov. 15—Intel Co-Founder Gordon E. Moore and his wife Betty have established a new multi-billion-dollar family foundation to focus on education, scientific research and the environment. The Gordon E. and Betty I. Moore Foundation will be headquartered in San Francisco, will function worldwide, and will begin operations early next year.**

If news outlets use nothing more than the lead, the essential information will be communicated broadly to the public. Even if the reader goes no further than the first paragraph, the essential information has been successfully delivered.

The Second Paragraph

Using the inverted pyramid style, the rest of the necessary information is now presented in descending order of importance.

The first paragraph is the lead. The second paragraph announces the man selected to build and lead the new Foundation. This is followed by an elaboration on the "what" and "why" of the Foundation. This is an opportunity to differentiate it from others of its type by focusing on what it expects to achieve and the potential benefits of those efforts.

> **Lewis W. Coleman will leave his post as chairman of BankAmerica Securities to become President of the new Foundation.**
>
> **Coleman said the Foundation will bring a "venture investment" philosophy to its grant-making. "We want to find good opportunities, which, though they may be a bit riskier, offer the possibilities of higher returns." He said, in general, these will be projects not ordinarily funded by conventional sources, such as government agencies. "We will look for those projects that can really make a substantial contribution to the quality of life and the health of the planet."**

Remaining Paragraphs

Coleman's credentials are established in the next two paragraphs, underscoring his ability to create and manage this unconventional "venture investment" approach, as well as his experience with educational and environmental matters.

> **Coleman brings to the position a reputation as an outside-the-box thinker with a record of personal involvement in environmental and educational matters and more than 30 years of experience as a successful executive. In addition to heading BankAmerica Securities, one of the country's leading investment-banking firms, he served as vice-chairman and chief financial officer of Bank of America, director of its World Banking Group, and chairman of the Credit Policy Committee of Wells Fargo Bank. He holds a degree in economics from Stanford University and serves on a number of boards.**

The next paragraph is intended to attract potential high-caliber employees to the exciting and rewarding jobs the Foundation will offer. It also helps further differentiate the Foundation in its intent to be aggressive in seeking worthy projects.

Coleman said staffing is already underway. "We hope to assemble a diverse group of thoughtful people who are passionate about making a difference. We want them out scouring the world for the best projects—not waiting for grant-seekers to come to us, but going out and finding what we ought to be supporting."

The next two paragraphs carry quotes from Coleman and Moore that further underscore the philosophy of the Foundation and Coleman's credentials. The "final word" lets readers know what to expect during the first year of operations and advises that active consideration of grants won't begin immediately.

"Gordon and Betty Moore have made an extremely generous gift to the world. We hope and expect that we can use this gift to make a difference on matters of fundamental importance to us all. I am very pleased to have been asked to head the Foundation and very excited about its potential," Coleman said.

Gordon Moore said, "The key to establishing the Foundation was finding the right person to build and run it. Lew brings the energy and excitement needed, along with outstanding executive credentials and passion for our areas of interest. Betty and I are thrilled that he is willing to take on this challenge."

Coleman anticipates the first year of operations to be largely occupied with organizing staff, setting grant request and reviewing procedures and becoming visible to people with the ideas and projects that should be brought to the Foundation's attention. Grants will be made as rapidly as qualifying projects are approved.

The Boilerplate

Almost all releases close with what is called "boilerplate," a paragraph containing the basic facts about the organization. It is included as a service to editors and reporters to save them time in looking up the particulars.

And that's it:

- two typewritten pages
- straight declarative sentences
- tight quotes used to illustrate or elaborate on statements of fact
- very limited use of superlatives (e.g., "extremely generous gift," "outstanding executive credentials")
- superlatives used only inside quotes, so it is clear they are the opinion of the speaker and not a general claim
- claims supported by facts
- no overstatements (overstatement kills credibility)

There is a strategy behind every sentence in the release. Nothing in it is gratuitous. This is a story that is intended to make something happen.

CLEARANCES

The next step in constructing a release is clearance.

Before any release moves publicly, it is necessary that the facts contained in it be vetted by the subject matter experts who provided them, and that the quotes be approved by the person(s) to whom they are attributed. In addition, depending upon the subject matter, the story might also require review and approval by the organization's attorneys.

The usual process involves providing a copy of the release in final draft form to the relevant parties, with a cover note asking for their comments. Two problems present themselves here. One is time. The other is the "everybody-is-a-writer" mentality.

If a release is ready to go, it should be moved as quickly as possible, which means that the people who have been given the release for comment need to respond almost immediately. Make that point clear in the cover note attached to the release. Use wording such as, "We plan to move this release at 10 a.m. tomorrow morning. Consequently, we need your comments or corrections back by the end of the day today. If we haven't heard from you by that time, we'll assume we have your okay. Thanks in advance for your cooperation." This usually does the trick.

The "everybody-is-a-writer" phenomenon poses a more difficult challenge. Many people in the review chain will consider themselves to be writers and can't resist the urge to "improve" the copy. The odds the copy will actually be improved in this way range from low to zero, but considerable time can be wasted trying to negotiate phrasing. If the ideas are indeed better, use them. If not, adopt the attorney's gambit of saying "comments noted" and put out the release as written.

DISTRIBUTION

The release, having been given a final proof-reading and cleared and vetted by all the necessary parties, is ready for distribution.

One of the fastest and most efficient methods of getting a release to the news media serving key constituent groups is through the use of commercial wire services such as BusinessWire and PR Newswire (www.businesswire.com and www.prnewswire.com). These organizations transmit releases electronically to major U.S. daily newspapers and radio and television newsrooms, as well as to the traditional newswire services, such as Associated Press, Dow-Jones, Bloomberg, Reuters and others.

In addition, these services have special circuits that cover media in specific geographic areas in this country and abroad, or particular areas of interest, such as the professional financial community or the high-tech or environmental communities. Lists can be tailored to reach almost any configuration of media almost anywhere. Internet distribution services provide similar access to Internet news outlets, blogs, Internet newsletters and special interest outlets.

Commercial wire services are fee-based operations. Typically, the user pays a small membership fee and then pays for each release sent by the agency. The fee is usually determined by the length of the story and the targeted circuit (e.g., full national coverage, San Francisco Bay Area, etc.)

Not all releases are candidates for commercial newswires. The service is most appropriately used by public companies when wide circulation and immediate attention to major breaking news is sought, or as a way to meet disclosure requirements. Some news organizations track these wire services only for the names of major and/or local companies they regularly follow and ignore all else. Some look only at datelines to determine if the story is local in the sense that it is about an organization in the publication's coverage area. Headlines, therefore, are enormously important. Be very thoughtful before committing your story to one of these newswires and almost never, unless you are a Fortune 500 company (and rarely then), use this method of distribution as your sole method. If you do file your release on BusinessWire or PR Newswire, a good practice is to email or call the reporters you think might be interested and alert them to your story.

If the story is important enough, all available methods of distribution should be used:

- commercial newswires and Internet services
- e-mail copies to key editors and writers by name (don't use FAXes to editors and writers—their FAX boxes are too full, the copy is inconvenient to work with, and in general, FAXes aren't checked regularly)
- e-mail or FAX copies to key constituents by name (do both to cover your bases, as your key constituents should be among the first to know)
- hand-delivered copies by messenger to key media contacts or key constituents as appropriate
- regular mail in cases where time isn't a factor and you want to be sure a hard copy of the release is on record with the recipient

In all instances, tailor the distribution to cover the constituents who are the targets of the exercise.

A SHORT RECAP

At this point, the basic types of releases, the uses for which they are intended and the standard format for each have been covered—including a generic template for writing a release. The only thing not yet covered is how to phrase the story—which, in the final analysis, is the actual writing. This is where you, as a writer, can really make an impact. It is your articulation of the facts as you understand them in the context of the results you are trying to achieve that gives the story the energy, importance and flair that makes it something worth reading. It is your singular view of the matter that draws and holds the reader.

Learning to do this, as has been noted, is accomplished mostly by doing—by studying how others do it and by trying to emulate best practice, and by working at your writing until it becomes sharp and telling.

The following guidelines, while covered previously, are worth repeating. They will be important to your final product.

- Pay attention to grammar, spelling and punctuation. Errors in any of these are unforgivable. If a writer can't get grammar, spelling or punctuation right, why should anyone expect that he portrayed the facts correctly? People who make such errors are either sloppy or lazy. Consequently, they have short-lived careers.
- Keep the writing simple. Say what you have to say as directly as you can.
- For news leads, try to work each of the Five Ws into the first sentence of the story and make that sentence the lead paragraph. If you can't manage to include all five, highlight the most important or most interesting and use it to fashion an attention-getting lead sentence. Incorporate the remaining key facts in a second sentence and make the lead a two-sentence paragraph.

- Use plain language and, for the most part, straight declarative sentences.
- Write tight. Keep the story as concise as you can. Take all the time and space needed to get the story told properly, but no more than that.
- Even if you are inordinately impressed with the subject, be careful of superlatives. Overstatement breeds disbelief. Flattering adjectives invite suspicion. If you must, use them in quotes attributable to someone referenced in the story. This makes them somewhat more acceptable.
- Make sure you understand what you are trying to explain to others.
- Question and examine and verify until you are satisfied that your writing is accurate and true. The two are not the same. Understand the difference.
- Do your best to make a valid story out of the subject at hand. If there is no story, say so.
- Be a believer. If you can't work up interest and enthusiasm for your subject, you won't be able to evoke those feelings from anyone else either.

INTERACTIVE EXERCISES CHAPTER 8

A Step-by-Step Template for Constructing a Release

Exercise One

You are the communications representative for Fair Oaks School District of Menifee County, Ohio. The district has just completed arrangements to introduce a new science instruction program at the elementary level that relies exclusively on local retired engineers and scientists who volunteer their time to teach. The volunteer program is part of a nationwide program called Science Rules, sponsored by the Industrial Scientists Association (ISA) in cooperation with local school boards. Science Rules programs are currently underway in 20 states. The objective of the program is to strengthen the science education offerings of local grade schools where budgets are strapped and qualified science teachers either overworked or unavailable. The end result sought by the program is new interest on the part of pre-teens in science and an increase in the number of students who chose science as a career. The benefits to business and industry and to the nation overall are considered enormous, as it will yield a larger, more competitive pool of engineering students. This is an important effort as America contends with Europe and Asia for leadership in science and technology. Getting kids interested in science and technology at an early age and keeping them motivated to learn and grow in the various disciplines from grade school through graduate school is vital. The Science Rules program is a key resource in helping achieve this goal. Menifee County will be the first county in the state to adopt the program.

The program will begin with special classes in computer technology being offered to sixth grade students once a week for eight weeks in schools in Jasper, Higgins, Fair Oaks and Lyle Creek. Six local retired engineers have been recruited to teach the classes and have completed an intense two-week ISA course on teaching science at the grade school level. Three of the engineers spent the majority of their careers with high-tech firms and three were specialists in computer applications for industry. There is no charge for their services, though travel expenses (i.e., mileage) are to be reimbursed by the school district. In addition, the district will cover the cost for instructional materials, Internet charges, audio-visual materials, etc.

You are to draft the announcement release. You will need quotes to enrich and expand the story. You may quote Vernon Riggs, superintendent of the Fair Oaks School Board; Jim Asper, president of ISA; Mary Mackson, principal of the Lyle Creek School, and/or Oscar Zampa, retired Microsoft hardware engineer and one of the volunteer teachers. You need not quote them all. Choose whom to quote and develop statements for them that best advance the objective of the story.

A. Develop the Fwsh for this story.
B. Using the structure in this chapter, write your release.

Exercise Two

A. The Moore Foundation release in this chapter begins with the name of the well-known man who is establishing the Foundation. The purpose of the Foundation just as easily could have been the focus. Which approach is stronger? In other words, which has more news value as a lead and is more likely to attract the reader?
B. Write the lead with the Foundation, not the founder, as the key focus.

Use the CD-ROM to check your work against our suggestions.

## CHAPTER NINE

TARGETING: GETTING TO THE RIGHT PEOPLE WITH THE RIGHT MESSAGE

Everything in this text is useless unless your message registers with those you need to reach.

This raises three questions:

1. Who are they?
2. How are they found?
3. How can they be reached?

In answering these questions, it is useful to adopt a coldly pragmatic view. Not every one needs to be reached. Not everyone's opinion is important. In the 21st century world of instantaneous, all pervasive communications, targeting is crucial. Very few organizations or institutions need to reach "the public," as that term is often used to mean almost everyone, almost everywhere. All institutions and organizations, however, need to reach their *constituents,* which in public relations means the people and groups whose "votes" are needed in order to succeed. These include employees, stockholders, customers, elected and appointed officials, local civic and social leaders, and business peers. These are the people whose actions and opinions make it possible for the organization to reach its goals, or put insurmountable roadblocks in its way.

WHERE ARE THEY?

How are they found?

Constituents are identified through research and analysis, most of which is surprisingly easy. For most organizations, the constituents are fairly obvious.

For example, the constituents for a publicly-traded profit-making enterprise include:

- People who own the company's stock or may buy it, those who lend it money or help it raise capital, and those whose recommendations directly affect its share price (stockholders, the professional financial community and security analysts);
- People who work for it or those whom it hopes to recruit (employees and potential employees);
- People who use its products and services and those who should (customers and potential customers);

- People who make the laws and write regulations that can affect its ability to operate and be profitable (members of local, state and federal legislative and regulatory bodies and their key staff members);
- Opinion leaders at the local, state and federal level;
- Special interest groups on whose areas of interest its activities intrude;
- Peers in business and industry (suppliers and competitors),
- Key media who report and comment on its activities to all the other key groups and that disseminate the organization's news rapidly and broadly to the people the organization is trying to reach.

Key constituents for a not-for-profit may vary slightly from this list. For example, a health-care organization's key constituents would be its members and providers, and for a charity, its existing and potential individual contributors. In all cases, the key constituents are the people and groups whose actions and opinions can help or hurt. Identifying these people by category (customers, opinion leaders) will be obvious with just a little thought. Those who aren't obvious are easily found by asking your client. They know who is important to them.

Consider that you represent the local school board and are promoting a bond issue to build a new grade school. Who is important? Parents of school-age children, naturally, but also critical are those voters over age 55, who may not have school-age children. This group typically represents the most active voting block and the more affluent residents of the area.

The people who *can* make a difference are those who *do* make the difference. They must not be overlooked.

GETTING TO THEM

How do you reach them?

The fast answer is through the mass commercial print and electronic media (newspapers, magazines, radio and television). These are the most rapid and most inexpensive conduits to get key information to both broad and targeted audiences. The challenge is that you have no control over how much of what you want to communicate actually gets used or how it's used. The editor or news director may decide to use the lead, part of the story, none of the story, or pick an element to highlight that which he finds interesting but is of only minor importance to your objective. This is what editing is all about. As chancy as this approach can sometimes be, disseminating information through the mass media was for years practically the only route to reach mass audiences—short of paying for an ad. This is not the case any longer. Today the advances of technology allow you to go directly to your key constituents—by name in many cases—with your full message unfiltered by a gatekeeper.

Through strategic use of the Internet, e-mail, Web sites, and special services offered by Internet distribution agencies, most key constituents can be reached directly and quickly with an unabridged message. In most cases, you don't even have to sacrifice graphic impact. This is an opportunity not to be overlooked.

MAKE IT PERSONAL

Good contact lists are key to working with both the traditional and the new electronic media.

It has been said that just as all winning politics are local, all effective communication is personal. To the extent possible, address your constituents by name. Make it personal.

Certainly all employees can be reached by name. The Human Resources department has a payroll or benefits list.

The secretary of the company has a list of stockholders (or use the annual report and 10-K mailing list).

The chief financial officer knows the key security analysts and the influential members of the professional financial community and how to reach them.

The sales and marketing groups will have a list of the most important customers.

The fund-raising managers in not-for-profits have a list of key donors and potential donors.

The community relations and governmental relations people have up-to-date lists of opinion leaders and important governmental contacts in the cities, states and countries where the organization operates. They also should have a list of the leaders of the most important special interest groups.

You, of course, have a listing of key media, to include writers, editors, columnists, on-air personalities and free-lancers.

THE HITTERS LIST

All together, these groups combine for a fairly significant "Hitters List," which is a way to think of your targeted constituents—heavy hitters, the people who make things happen.

Not every constituent is on all the lists all the time. Lists are constructed for specific purposes. The list for a new product introduction would be different from one built to raise understanding and visibility for a plant expansion, or to explain a position on an environmental issue. Each list is tailored to achieve a specific result.

The sources for assembling these lists are almost endless—industry trade associations, professional organizations, governmental directories, local Chambers of Commerce or Convention and Visitors Bureaus, alumni associations, fraternal organizations, civic and service clubs, directories like *Who's Who*, and many others. The point is to utilize resources that help to identify key people by name.

Mass media distribution lists will be needed as well. These lists contain the names and addresses of writers and editors at media outlets, such as *The Wall Street Journal* and *Business Week;* the wire services, such as Associated Press, Reuters and Bloomberg; the local area daily and weekly newspapers; selected radio and TV outlets, and trade publications read by the target audiences. *Bacon's, Burrell's, Editor & Publisher Yearbook, Broadcasting and Cable Yearbook,* and several other special directories have full information on contacts for virtually all print and electronic media in the U.S. and abroad.

As with the "Hitters List," each media list should be constructed specifically for the targeted constituent group—environmentalists, seniors, soccer moms, farmers. Don't assume one list fits all. It won't.

INTERACTIVE EXERCISES CHAPTER 9

Targeting: Getting to the Right People with the Right Message

Exercise One

You are the public information officer for Edwards University and you're handling the "Edwards Drops Football" story outlined earlier. Construct the "Hitters List" for this story. You don't need the actual names of people, but the categories of people you need to reach (concentrate on those whose actions and opinions could make a difference). Keep foremost in mind the first W in the Fwsh: Why Am I Doing This?

Exercise Two

What reference sources would you use to assemble a list of local print and broadcast media?

Exercise Three

Go online and check out the distribution lists offered by BusinessWire and PR Newswire (www.businesswire.com and www.prnewswire.com). Also search for Internet news release distribution services.

A. Would you use BusinessWire or PR Newswire for the Edwards University story? Why?
B. How about an Internet news release service? Why?
C. Would you use any of the above (or all) for the Moore Foundation story? Why?

Use the CD-ROM to compare answers.

BEYOND THE BASICS: PIECES THAT SELL, PERSUADE, INFORM AND MOTIVATE

## CHAPTER TEN

OP-ED PIECES, SIGNED ARTICLES AND LETTERS AS TACTICAL TOOLS

The "persuasion kit" has many tools. Among the most effective are op-eds, signed articles and letters.

Op-eds are the opinion pieces that play opposite the editorial page in most major newspapers, hence "op-ed." Almost all papers of any size have them. The pages are intended to offer a platform from which opinions and arguments in favor of this or that cause can be voiced, or where issues of note and consequence to the readership can be discussed. Op-eds offer a wonderful opportunity for partisans.

Since op-eds are clearly opinion pieces, the extent to which they carry credibility and are effective depends on the reputation and credentials of the author, and, of course, the "believability" of the argument.

USE SPARINGLY

Op-eds should be used sparingly. Save them for situations when you have something important to say about an issue of significance. A point made in an op-ed piece appearing in a respected publication gives it a significance and substance that doesn't flow from any other placement.

The writing is a challenge. Typically the writer has only 900 to 1200 words in which to make the case. The points must be thoughtful and provocative and the development of the argument authoritatively elegant. As such, the focus on the "what-do-they-need-to-know-or-believe-in-order-to-come-to-the-desired-conclusions" exercise is paramount. The premium is on spare writing and on compelling reasoning.

When writing an op-ed:

· Use a strong opening that will attract the reader's attention.
· Get to the point right away. Don't try to slide into your message with a slow build-up.
· Lead with a single provocative line or a short punchy paragraph that highlights the issue.
· Write it in the tone you would use if you were communicating with a reasonable, but skeptical, friend whose opinion you value.
· Lay out your arguments in a conversational voice, fitting them together to lead logically and with impact to a conclusion that supports the basic premise.

To place an op-ed piece:

- Contact the page editor with a short letter or email that summarizes the piece you are offering.
- Describe its importance and interest to the paper's readers.
- Outline the basic point(s) the piece will make.
- Underscore the credentials and expertise of the person whose name will head the article.

If the editor is interested, then produce the piece.

Be sure the right person has been selected as the author. He or she must have the experience, position and credentials that reassure readers the author is knowledgeable and authoritative.

Only rarely will the credited author actually have written the piece. He or she will provide the information, structure the argument, even do a rough draft, but the finished writing normally is left to a professional.

Op-eds are exclusive. Don't try to place the same one in different publications. If the editor decides not to take your offer, you're perfectly free to go elsewhere. And you should, in that case, but one publication at a time.

Following is an example of an op-ed in the typical format. This one is intended to help calm a potentially inflammable situation. It is unusual in that it relies heavily on reciting the opposition's complaints to build credibility, before getting to the action the article hopes to inspire. Although risky, this approach can be effective in the hands of a seasoned professional.

For Open Forum
The Louisville Courier-Journal

By Ted Phillips
1200 words

Prelude to a Requiem.

Upon the passing of the great, it is customary that a requiem be offered. One should be said for Elkhorn Distilleries. It is dead, and by the time this latest round of job cuts, 500 is the estimate, is completed, the company we've all known for so many years will be gone forever.

To refresh your memory, Natumi, of Tokyo, and Elkhorn Distilleries announced last spring an agreement to merge. The two distilling giants were to come together, pool their talent and resources, become a marketing behemoth, and do grand things for shareholders, customers and employees. A "merger of equals" it was called.

At the time, the business case for the merger seemed a stretch. It is hard to fathom why Elkhorn, given the reputation of its products and the strength of its marketing, needed Natumi in order to be successful in the new millennium. Elkhorn was one of the most honored names in distilling anywhere in the world. With its dominant position in the Eastern markets, it owned the best franchise in the business. It already had a nationwide distribution. It had a strong international position and reputation, a solid management team with excellent credentials and proven records, a loyal and dedicated work force, and was diversifying into allied fields (fertilizers, stock feed) in an intelligent manner.

All of which is to say that Elkhorn seemed to have plenty of muscle and sufficient resources to make it on its own quite well. Wall Street thought well of its prospects and its performance and its stock price was hovering near historic highs.

That was almost a year ago. Today, Elkhorn shares, which were trading at a little over $45 at the time of the merger, are around $20 a share. There has been no noticeable increase in the share of market that Elkhorn commands. Sales are flat.

Elkhorn was a key employer in this region and a strong contributor to the health and economies of the communities in which it has operations. Its people, whether executive manager or bottling-line worker, were involved and cared. They made a difference.

Natumi can never play the role Elkhorn played in its communities. It won't want to. It won't be able to. It doesn't have the mind-set for it. For Natumi, Kentucky is just another plant location; Louisville is just another city. It isn't home. It isn't where the company grew up and has roots and memories and commitment.

Natumi has a different culture and a different leadership. Its approach has worked elsewhere. It may work here. I'm told that business is brisk and customer retention is high. I wish them success. They won and the winner gets to make the decisions.

But the going is tough and the outlook uncertain. The folk from Natumi, and the Elkhorn managers and employees who survived the cut and who are trying to run the company, have a very big problem before them. Facing the prospect of yet another round of layoffs, the mood of the community is turning ugly. There has been talk of a boycott, picketing, torch-light demonstrations in front of executives' homes. These may help assuage some of the anger and grief at the merger, but they won't half solve the problem. The problem is that Elkhorn-Natumi needs to get this merger successfully digested and start the company moving upward again. For all of us, the reasonable thing to do is to get behind them. The company is still providing jobs and paying taxes and mailing out dividend checks. With success, they will provide more of each—to the benefit of all concerned . . . employees, customers, shareholders, and the community.

We need to be smart enough to realize this and pragmatic enough to try to help them be successful—assuming they play fair and recognize their responsibilities to the community.

The Economist magazine, in a recent article on the success of big mergers, noted that "major mergers are like second marriages, a triumph of hope over experience." We all know of second marriages that are very successful. This can be one, too. If we don't meddle.

Ted Phillips

Mr. Phillips, a Louisville resident, was Executive Vice President, Marketing, for Elkhorn Distilleries. He left the company shortly after the merger with Natumi to form a consultancy. Natumi is one of his clients.

SIGNED ARTICLES

Signed articles, or by-liners, are used principally in support of marketing programs or in a positioning effort to create interest in an idea, or a place or a project, or to help build a particular individual's reputation or persona. Signed articles cover a matter of importance, authored by an expert on the subject.

The typical placement is in trade publications serving a market of particular interest to the client, such as *Engineering News Record* or *Health Facilities Management* magazine, or in technical or professional journals, such as *The Journal of the American Society of Information Science and Technology.*

Like the "pitch" for an op-ed story, the approach to the editor is made through a short query by letter or email describing the piece and detailing the credentials of the author. The story idea has to be good and the query letter first rate. If the editor accepts, you develop the piece as you would any other feature article.

The exception here is for articles intended for certain trade or technical journals. These publications often have a style of their own that must be followed. For these specialized publications, the signed author is frequently the actual author. Your role is essentially that of an editor, making sure the story is suitable and ready for the intended publication.

Reprints for Cross-Marketing

Delivering reprints of signed articles to selected constituents can be a very effective marketing tool, expanding the reach of the piece far beyond the publication's readership.

The tactic of cross-marketing op-eds and signed articles is very important. By sending reprints or copies to selected readers who are important to your effort, you insure they have an opportunity to see the piece, whether or not they have read the publication in which it appears. By bringing it directly to the attention of important constituents, specifically those on your "hitters list," the reach and impact of the article is magnified significantly. Sometimes, the cross-marketing effort is more important than the original placement.

The article below is an example of a signed article targeted to a "trade" publication, in this case, a publication serving the banking industry.

By Lew Coleman
Vice Chairman, BankAmerica Corporation

For The New England Banker

NEW ENGLAND SHOULD SETTLE FOR NOTHING LESS

Sometime within the next two weeks, the future of the New Bank of New England, the New Connecticut Bank & Trust Company, and the New Maine National Bank will be decided.

These are the present components of the Bank of New England Corporation, which failed in January of this year, and which were taken over by the Federal Deposit Insurance Corporation. The FDIC has been seeking a buyer to take on the responsibility of reshaping these institutions and turning them once again into a positive force in their communities and in the region. Three organizations have confirmed their willingness to do so: the Bank of Boston; a consortium composed of KKR, the country's leading leveraged buy-out firm and Fleet/Norstar Financial Group, and BankAmerica.

The FDIC is evaluating the various bids now and is expected to announce its selection early next week. While the decision as to who will be awarded the bid is of considerable importance to the customers and employees of the failed institutions, it is of equal, perhaps greater, importance to the communities these banks serve and the New England economy overall.

Strong, well-managed banks provide the fuel that allows businesses to prosper, jobs to be created, homes to be bought and educations to be got. Strong, well managed banks help make strong and healthy communities.

In that context, what is at issue in the New Bank of New England case is not just the matter of the highest qualified bid, nor the question of whether an "in-region" vs. "outside" winner would be "better" for New England.

Also at issue are the immediate capital resources the successful bidder is prepared and able to bring to the region to help stimulate the weakened economy; the depth and experience of its management talent, and the probability that the successful bidder can, and will, build a strong and well-managed institution committed to its communities and to New England for the long term.

BankAmerica has the resources, the management, and the commitment.

The corporation has both the capital and the management experience to start working on the turn-around right away. We're no stranger to turn-arounds. When BofA acquired Seafirst (Washington state's largest bank), it was on the verge of collapse. Today, it is the state's most profitable bank, its largest holder of deposits, and the state's leading lender.

With more than $6.4 billion in shareholder equity, BankAmerica is considered among the best capitalized of the nation's big banks. Our Community Reinvestment Act record earned the highest rating possible from the Federal rating agency responsible for monitoring how banks perform in their communities. Only 8% of U.S. banks achieved that rating.

And the corporation's marketing abilities and its focus on customer service has won it either first or second place in most of the markets it serves.

These are among the strengths that BankAmerica would bring to New England.

Clearly, if BankAmerica is the winning bidder, we will be a strong competitor. Heightened competition should work to the consumers' benefit, and in the long run, should help ensure that New Englanders have access to the best and most efficient banking services in the country.

For BankAmerica's part, we are eager to help achieve that goal and to play an important role in the realization of the opportunity the region holds. Whoever the winning bidder may be, New England should settle for nothing less.

LETTERS

One other type of special writing should be considered here: letters.

Letters deserve far more attention in public relations programs as a tactical device than they usually receive. Consider "Letters To The Editor." Because these letters are usually in reply to an item that recently appeared, they offer an opportunity for an almost immediate response to a matter important to the client. But letters to the editor handled in the ordinary way have four inherent drawbacks:

- They offer very little space in which to make your case—typically 200 to 300 words or less.
- Even if the case is well made within this space constraint, the editor may choose not to publish it.
- If the letter is published, the editor has the right to edit and shorten it, possibly leaving out what you consider the most important points.
- If the letter is published, many of the constituents most important to you may not see it. They may not read the paper or magazine that day, or if they do read the publication that day, they may not notice your letter.

Even so, if handled with a little creativity, a letter to the editor can be just as effective as an op-ed piece. In certain situations, it can be more effective. This results when a letter to the editor is used as a platform for taking your message *directly* to your key constituents. In this case, whether or not the publication uses the letter is relatively unimportant. What is important is that you make your case in the *form* of a letter to the editor. With that letter in hand, you can make sure it gets the attention of your key constituents.

Reach your key constituents by delivering a copy of the letter directly to them. You don't send it blind or unexplained, of course. It must be sent with a cover letter, explaining that the enclosure is a copy of a letter recently sent to the editor of (whatever publication) which you hope will be published soon and in its entirety. But you realize that such letters sometimes don't make it into print, or if they do, they are sometimes considerably shortened to fit available space. Your cover letter goes on to say that, realizing this, you want to make sure your constituent, *because this is an important matter and because his or her opinions are important to you,* has the opportunity to read the letter in its entirety.

This is often a more effective approach than writing directly to your key constituents. It has the appeal of giving them an advance look at a message you are hoping will be published for widespread dissemination without coming across as special pleading to a select audience. It also frees you of the 200–300-word space constraint. Since your basic objective is to get your message to your key constituents rather than to see the letter actually published, you can forgo the space constraints on regular letters to the editor and take all the space necessary to make your case fully. The message still must be concise, but it needn't be overly abbreviated. You do, of course, hope the letter will be published. Regardless, you still send a copy with a cover letter, because not everyone reads every issue of the newspaper or magazine every day. You don't want your message missed by those most important to your organization's success.

Letters also provide an effective tool for creating news without actually issuing a news release.

Let's say we are Edwards University again and we want to avoid a high visibility release that would automatically attract attention, but we do want get the word out about the change in our sports program. Most importantly, we want to do so in a way that positions the decision as a reasonable response to an unavoidable situation.

So we write a letter to our students and alumni. We do this, because a letter format offers us the opportunity to do things that we cannot do in a news release format. We can explain our rationale. We can offer opinions. We can draw conclusions.

In the letter, we announce the decision, explain the reasons the action is necessary and explain the board of regent's rationale. We express regret, but we underscore the strong conviction that this is the right course for the university at this time. Most importantly, we reinforce the university's commitment to providing a superior liberal arts education as its core mission.

Rather than issue a formal release, we send a copy of the letter to all relevant media with a cover note reading something to the effect that, 'We thought you might be interested in a message we are sending to our students and alumni today." Since this is a copy of a communication between a university and its students and alumni, it takes on a special aura. It's not exactly a private conversation, but it isn't a widely public one either. The media is allowed to be privy to what the university is saying about its action to those it impacts most. Nothing earth-shaking. The sky isn't falling. The world isn't ending. The university is just taking a responsible, necessary action and is giving its people details.

With this sort of handling, the odds are that the university will get a more responsible, less sensational treatment than would be likely with the more typical news release.

There are numerous of ways to use this technique in matters involving all your constituents—customers, employees, even shareholders. When and as the technique is used, make sure the letter reads like a letter. It should be conversational, straightforward and personal.

To follow is an example of a Letter to the Editor responding to a critical piece about a particular company's product. In this case, getting the letter to the company's key customers and certain influential high-tech trade journal writers was more important than the letter actually being published in *The Economist*, so copies were sent with a cover letter to those contacts at the same time the letter was mailed to the magazine. Note: the salutation on the actual letter to the editor is always addressed to "The Editor," not to the editor by name. The envelope, however, is addressed to the editor by name and at the appropriate address.

EVERYWHERE, INC.

The Editor
THE ECONOMIST

Dear Editor,

Regarding the "Face Value" column item titled *One Hand Clapping* in the June 2nd issue, we appreciate the recognition of Everywhere, Inc.'s leading position in the worldwide handheld computer industry and the author's interest in our success. While we can't agree with all the observations (who can in any article?), they certainly fall within the realm of fair comment and we accept them in the positive spirit in which we are sure they were intended.

But there are two small quibbles—for the record. As matter of fact, and record, Everywhere outsells Springboard on the order of ten to one in both unit volume and dollar sales and we have about two-thirds of the U.S. market share (according to the latest weekly figures from NPD Intellect), far outstripping any of our competitors and continuing to underscore our position as the market leader. Our new products, specifically the new x2000 series (color and black and white), which has been on the market only a few months and which is selling quite well, gives users, through its dual expansion architecture, a flexibility and reach simply not available in any comparable product. Which fact, we suggest, amounts to a bit more than simply the addition of an expansion slot like Springboard's. This is not to belittle Springboard. We think they have a fine product and we wish them success, too. After all, we license our operating system to them.

We do appreciate that we have challenges and that time, of course, is of the essence. Where there is challenge, there is opportunity. We understand both and are confident we can rise above the one and maximize the other.

Respectfully,

Jamie Rising
Manager, International Sales

The next letter is an example of one done in lieu of issuing a release. Rather than making a formal announcement of the start of a fund-raising campaign in a not entirely favorable environment, a copy of a letter being sent to a broad segment of the community is also sent to local media. The letter is used to impart both the basic information and rationale in expectation of stimulating responsible coverage. The letter allows the writer to address questions (and potential criticisms) not typically addressed in an announcement release and provides the opportunity to position the action more effectively than might be done with attributed quotes. A cover letter would accompany this piece, explaining what it is and offering to provide more information.

East Ridge Diocese
Pine Glade, Michigan

A Letter to the People of the Diocese and Its Friends

After long study and much debate, a group representing all parts of the diocese and a few of the diocese's friends have come together to raise, with your help, a new diocesan cathedral.

We have been without such a place for too long. Our old cathedral was lost in the fire of 2002. During that time, the diocese has been homeless. Now, in the early years of the new millennium—a time of unprecedented change, yet a time with unprecedented opportunities for openness and inclusion, we need a home where we can come together to work on our problems, realize our opportunities, and celebrate our faith as a community of the whole. The new cathedral will provide that place.

This is a monumental undertaking. We need to raise monies on the order of several hundreds of millions of dollars. The Bishop is adamant that the cathedral must be funded by private donations exclusive of the diocesan budget and accounted for separately and transparently. Times are hard now and the economic outlook uncertain. Raising this amount of money in this environment will be a difficult task.

But it will be worth it.

Throughout history, cathedrals have been the treasured symbols of the force of faith and testaments to the creative reach of the human mind. They have enriched their communities with their beauty. Their presence has been a source of pride for believers and non-believers alike. And their services have benefited all.

The new cathedral will be such a place. Soaring 15 stories, with a roof that opens to the sky, capable of seating 1800 people, and designed to simulate two hands clasped in prayer, it will be a landmark for the city and an architectural treasure for the entire area. It will be ecumenical in practice, encouraging interaction with all faiths and stimulating understanding among all. It will host educational, civic, and cultural events, becoming a community as well as a religious resource. And it will serve as the parish church for the residents of downtown, a large and culturally mixed community, which once had a parish of its own, but has not since the fire.

A basic question, of course, is a cathedral really needed and needed now? Can't we keep making do as we have been doing for the past three years? The answer is yes, the cathedral is really needed, and needed now—for the health and future of the diocese and for the many benefits both economic and social it will bring to the community and the area.

We need your help and support to make this a reality. If you have questions, ask us. If you want more information, contact us. If you can support us, please do.

Sincerely,

Bailey Connaught
Chairman
The Pine Glade Cathedral Project

For all these—op-ed, signed articles, letters—here are a few guidelines:

1. An easy style is better than a rigid one,
2. Humor works better than rancor,
3. Reason works better than bombast,
4. Shorter is better than longer and
5. Preaching or ranting is ill-advised.

Finally, here is an example of the way a letter, whether to the editor, the organization's most important client, or a prospective employer, should be formatted. In this case, the letter is addressed to the president of a public relations agency.

James Brody
Principal

Tuesday, September 09, 2004

Reed Byrum
Strategic Communications Counsel
2800 Waymaker Way, Ste. 59
Austin, TX 78746

Reed,

Just a short note.

Excellent session last evening. I'm a little embarrassed to say I didn't realize the thrust or extent of the program for PRSA you have underway, but am very impressed. It seems exactly what's needed and I hope the direction and momentum are maintained when you roll out of the chair.

I imagine there are a lot of senior (read that in terms of both age and position) people like me, who share, if not a collective ignorance of the program, at least an unfortunate lack of awareness of same. Yes, I get the printed material, but no I don't often read it. I'm sure that doesn't surprise you. We're all a little lazy and/or focused on our priorities of the moment.

I don't have any ideas about what is to be done about this, but all of us ought to be strongly behind this program and be giving it our active support, because I agree with you that the time is exactly right for the function to show its muscle and move into more influential space. To the extent this is seen as a problem by the leadership, I'm sure you and the oncoming slate of new officers will figure out what to do about it.

Best regards,

James Brody
Public Relations and Communications
725 Ocala Drive
Key West, FL 33040
(305) 276-1000 / Fax (305) 276-1001

INTERACTIVE EXERCISES CHAPTER 10

Op-ed Pieces, Signed Articles and Letters as Tactical Tools

Exercise One

Assume your client is Edwards University and you want to promote Edwards' commitment to academic excellence as a marketing tool to help attract new students, and, indirectly, to build Edwards' reputation in the overall national academic community. One of the tools we decide to use is an op-ed piece targeted for the *Chicago Tribune*. The piece is to be carried under the byline of James L. Considine, president of the University. Using the University's recent decision to drop intercollegiate football and rededicate itself to academic excellence, develop two ideas on op-ed subjects you think help make the University's case and write the opening paragraph for each.

Exercise Two

Edwards University is your client and you have decided to use the letter technique to make the University's case to students and alumni on the decision to drop football and as a device by which to break the story to the media. Write the first two paragraphs of the letter. The letter will go out over the signature of President James L. Considine.

Use the CD-ROM to compare ideas.

## CHAPTER ELEVEN

CONVENTIONAL LETTERS, NEWSLETTERS AND BROCHURES

Among the most common public relations tools are letters, newsletters and brochures. They can range from technical to conversational pieces, from standardized to specialized, with purposes dictating their tone.

Letters may be one-to-one or group communication. When they appear on letterhead, they reflect the company's image and carry a note of credibility. Letterhead carries the company's "face." Standards and guidelines for use of letterhead should be set by the company.

Letters should follow standard format for business style. For example:

Date
(skip down four lines)
Name and title of recipient
Company name
Street address
City, State Zip code
(skip down two spaces)
Dear _____,
(skip down one space)
Introduction
(double-space between paragraphs)
Body
Conclusion, with action statement
(skip down two lines)
Sincerely,
(skip down four lines to allow space for signature)
Name
Title

Letter recipients may be addressed in the salutation by first name, or with honorific titles: Ms., Mr., Mrs., Dr., etc., depending upon the relationship to the writer. Avoid using "Dear Sir or Dear Madam," preferring instead to personalize with the individual's name.

In the introductory paragraph, do *not*:

- say, "I am writing this letter . . ." That's obvious.
- introduce yourself: "I am Kim Hall." Your name will appear at the bottom of the letter, so omit the obvious.

Except in unusually complicated matters, try to limit the letter to a single page. Introduce the topic, provide information, and end with an "action statement" that gives the recipient a step or steps to take (e.g., "Please feel free to contact me at 1-800-555-5555," or "I look forward to hearing from you at your earliest convenience," or "Let me know, if I may provide additional information," etc.).

NEWSLETTERS

Newsletters are among the most versatile tools available for both internal and external communications. Organizations target them to customers, shareholders, community leaders and employees. They are done both in print and electronic formats, and are a favored method for getting timely information to key constituents on a regular basis at minimum cost. Most print newsletters are produced in $8\frac{1}{2}$ by 11-inch format with short one- or two-paragraph stories under catchy headlines. They run in length from as little as one page to as many as four pages front and back. Most have very clean graphic design, though some are no more pretentious than a computer-generated page in simple Times New Roman or Garamond type face. Increasingly, electronic newsletters delivered via email or made available for access on an organization's Web site are becoming the method of choice for regular communications with key constituents. For either the print or electronic version, the KISS (Keep It Short and Simple) rule strongly applies.

Employee newsletters are used to:

- Communicate necessary company information,
- Recognize the good work of employees or members,
- Highlight special programs,
- Promote future events,
- Explain policy,
- Engender cooperation,
- Announce appointments, elections, etc.

Newsletters for external audiences are designed to:

- Deliver important and timely information about matters important to the constituent and to the organization,
- Keep customers and potential customers informed on new products and new technological developments,
- Promote services and events,
- Provide a credible communications device for staying in regular contact with the organization's important clients.

Desktop publishing has made it easy for newsletters to be produced in-house on a regular weekly, monthly or quarterly schedule. In order to have impact, frequency is important.

In producing newsletters:

- Keep the focus on providing information the reader will find timely, useful and interesting, but in the context of the overall objective set for the publication.
- Make it readable and interesting to the eye.
- Select a readable type style and stick to it! Using multiple type faces gives the newsletter an amateurish look.
- Use photos carefully. The usual newsletter format doesn't lend itself easily to photo display. The page is too small. Unless the shot is excellent and makes a point important to the story, or is an important or interesting story in itself, resist the temptation to dress up the page with photos. A photo isn't worth a thousand words. Look at a photo of the Declaration of Independence and then read it. See which you think has the most impact. If you do use photos of people, make sure you select shots in which the individuals are recognizable and identifiable. Charts and graphs, on the other hand, are good to use. They tell a tight story that can be grasped right away, and they have an added advantage of looking authoritative.
- "Write it right and write it tight!" Newsletters have limited space. Keep articles short. This is where the KISS rule applies.
- Check spelling and grammar. The newsletter represents the organization, and mistakes should not be tolerated.

Following is an example of one type of newsletter—a four-color piece done by the Navy League for its members.

NAVY LEAGUE of the UNITED STATES

Supplement to Sea Power

The Navy LEAGUER

VOLUME 10 • NUMBER 1 • February 2005

Ask not what the sea services can do for you, but what you can do for the sea services!

The 2005 Legislative Initiative

By Jeremy Miller
NLUS Legislative Affairs

In recent years, considerable progress has been made in the Navy League's overall legislative affairs program. At the same time, however, critical legislative affairs requirement are needed to achieve our essential mission of educating Members of Congress on the needs of the sea services.

With the combination of the post cold war cutbacks over several years and the recent war on terror, our sea services face unprecedented challenges that need the strongest possible support of the Navy League's legislative affairs capabilities. These challenges include such issues as the significant decline in the U.S. fleet size to unacceptable levels; less than satisfactory funding for the Coast Guard; and the continuing decline in U.S. flagged merchant ships, among many other important issues.

The "Grass Roots Legislative Transformation Initiative" has been launched to increase Navy League legislative affairs activities sufficiently to close the "gap" identified above, thereby bringing the Navy League's educational efforts for Members of Congress to the level needed in today's environment. Perhaps the single most important element of the project is to increase the involvement by Regions, Areas, and Councils in legislative affairs activities.

To achieve our legislative initiative, the appointment of a Regional Vice President for Legislative Affairs in each of the Navy League's 14 domestic regions has been made. Reporting to the Region President with a "dotted line" relationship to the National Vice President for Legislative Affairs, the individuals who fill these new posts will play a primary part in our future success. They will bring local Navy League people together with selected members of Congress to carry out our support mission. The Regional Vice Presidents will serve as the experts in their regions for grass roots visits and communications; conduct an annual training session on legislative affairs based on national guidelines and materials; and work with area and council officers in the region to ensure they are receiving appropriate information and support on legislative affairs. They also will recommend annual legislative affairs awards from the region using national criteria.

For more information on the Grass Roots Legislative Initiative, Please visit the Navy League's website at: http://www.navyleague.org/legislative_affairs/

See page 10 for a listing of Regional Vice Presidents appointed.

Inside this Issue

Your PR Team

2 Member Tips

4 Council News

7 JROTC In Key West

www.navyleague.org

BROCHURES

Like newsletters, brochures are an important and versatile tool useful for purposes ranging from new product introductions to educating the public on environmental and economic issues. Most of the tips that apply to writing newsletters also apply to producing brochures. Be clear on the objective, or that which you want to achieve with the brochure. Once that determination is made, prepare a budget and do a mock-up before writing the copy. Since space is limited and the packaging so important, tailoring the copy to fit the design is often a good idea.

Tri-fold brochures are popular, because the design is easy to manage and the finished product fits nicely into a standard envelope for mailing. One-page flyers have the advantage of serving as mini-posters, as well as mailers. Weigh the advantages, with the objective in mind.

To follow is a typical tri-fold. This example, done for The Birch Aquarium at the Scripps Institution of Oceanography, shows the outside of the tri-fold and a page with directions and general information.

INTERACTIVE EXERCISES CHAPTER 11

Conventional Letters, Newsletters and Brochures

Exercise One

Select any brochure done by a university or college and write a brief synopsis and critique, using the guidelines from the chapter.

Exercise Two

Recast the "A Letter to the People of the Diocese" from the last chapter into a one paragraph story for a newsletter done by the Diocese that circulates to the pastors of all its churches.

Use the CD-ROM to compare answers.

## CHAPTER TWELVE

MEDIA KITS AND FACT SHEETS

Since a primary function of public relations is to assist reporters in doing their jobs, Media Kits, otherwise known as "Press Kits," are effective tools of the trade. Not only are they a service to the media, they also serve to attract and focus attention on a product or an event by providing news and information in visually appealing and functionally efficient packages. They are often used as the "take-away" package at major news conferences, so that media have complete and in-depth information in a handy file that can be kept for future reference. They are sometimes distributed as a stand-alone package accompanying a major news release, when a media conference isn't being staged.

Contents should be tailored to the purpose of the kit. General media kits should include:

- History of company
- Biographical information on CEO and others, as appropriate
- Fact sheet
- News release
- Business card of contact person

Then, depending on the purpose, such as introducing a new product or service, add:

- Media advisory
- Product or service description
- History of product or service, the invention, discovery or origin, etc.
- Biographical notes on the principals involved
- Newsletter and/or brochure
- Photographs, art-work or other illustration

Be sure to tailor the content to the medium for which it is intended. The needs of print, radio and television are different, so the kits should be fashioned to present your story in the most effective manner and with the content shaped to suit the particular medium. For example, you should offer short releases and strong visuals for television, and perhaps 30-second taped sound-bites for radio. This can mean three versions of the same media kit, but the time and expense involved in tailoring is worthwhile if the product or event justifies the effort.

Media kits are only useful if recipients open them. The subject matter and content must be so compelling or the design of the kit be so creative and interesting that the recipient can't resist looking inside. A high premium is placed on creativity in the design of the kit. Depending upon the budget, covers range from colored file-folders to four-color designs with special pockets for information. Elaborate covers for companies such as Disney have gone so far as to include a computer chip, with music or sound effects, or 'pop-up' designs for special effects.

Some fundamental pointers to keep in mind when considering design are these:

- Stick to standard file-folder size, since the kits will be placed on a shelf or in a filing cabinet.
- Include the company's identity on the cover.
- Avoid white, as fingerprints will spoil the cover as it is handled.
- Design should cover both the front and back, because the kit has a 50-50 chance of landing on either side on the reporter's desk. (It costs no more to use a wrap-around design, so go for it!)
- Put your "best foot forward" on the cover, and make sure it is appropriate for the image of the company.

Media kits recast as information kits are useful with other groups. Stockholders, new employees, prospects, and others may need the information presented in the kits for background. Quite frequently information kits are tailored with these uses in mind and are effective tools.

The creative team, to include artists, photographers and graphic designers, should work closely with the writers to package the information in the most attractive and accessible manner.

Notice the visual appeal of the cover of this media kit from Birch Aquarium of the Scripps Institution of Oceanography, followed by examples of some of the materials included in the kit (a release, a media advisory and reprint of an article) and how they all tie together.

BIRCH aquarium

at SCRIPPS INSTITUTION OF OCEANOGRAPHY

* UNIVERSITY OF CALIFORNIA, SAN DIEGO

UNIVERSITY OF CALIFORNIA, SAN DIEGO

SCRIPPS INSTITUTION OF OCEANOGRAPHY

BIRCH AQUARIUM AT SCRIPPS NEWS

CONTACT: Jessica Demian
or Cindy Clark
858/534-3624
scrippsnews@ucsd.edu
FOR RELEASE: January 14, 2005

Tide-Pool Adventures with the Birch Aquarium at Scripps
Scripps Institution of Oceanography/UCSD

As shorter days are upon us this winter, we lose a little daylight in the afternoons, but we're gaining beach! Read below about the wonders of tidepooling. Call the Birch Aquarium to find out about naturalist-guided tours of the coastline or stop by the Birch Aquarium Bookshop for field guides. *We're your ocean connection!*

LIFE AT THE EDGE OF LAND AND SEA

The coming and going of tides is orchestrated by the gravitational pulls of the sun and moon. From late fall to early spring in southern California, minus tides (tides that recede below zero tide level) occur in daylight hours. Minus tides of one foot or greater present the best opportunities for viewing tide pools teeming with marine life. Now is the season for tidepooling!

You will be delighted by the variety of creatures along the strip of shoreline alternately covered and uncovered by the changing tides. Hermit crabs, sea anemones, sea stars, barnacles, and perhaps even a two-spotted octopus are just a few of the many species that might be discovered in the nooks and crannies of tide pools. Many of these creatures shelter under rocks or bury in the sand; some can hide in plain sight thanks to camouflage. Like a hidden puzzle, you must look carefully to discover a tide pool's treasures.

- over -

SCRIPPS COMMUNICATIONS
9500 Gilman Drive, Dept 0233 • La Jolla, California • 92093-0233 • Tel: (858) 534-3624 • Fax: (858) 534-5306
Web: aquarium.ucsd.edu • scrippsnews.ucsd.edu • E-mail: scrippsnews@ucsd.edu
UCSD

UNIVERSITY OF CALIFORNIA, SAN DIEGO

SCRIPPS INSTITUTION OF OCEANOGRAPHY

BIRCH AQUARIUM AT SCRIPPS **NEWS**

CONTACT: Jessica Demian
or Cindy Clark
858/534-3624
scrippsnews@ucsd.edu
FOR RELEASE: February 24, 2005

MEDIA ADVISORY

Local Students Compete in Ocean Sciences Bowl at Scripps
Scripps Institution of Oceanography, University of California, San Diego

WHO: Seventeen teams from local high schools will compete in Surf Bowl 2005, the regional competition for the National Ocean Sciences Bowl (NOSB).

WHAT: Surf Bowl is a fast-paced academic bowl in which student teams attempt to answer questions about ocean life and the marine environment in a "Jeopardy-style" match. Winners of the regional competition will advance to the national championship in Mississippi in April.

WHEN: **Saturday, February 26, 9 a.m. to 4 p.m.**
Competition rounds begin at 9 a.m.

WHERE: Scripps Institution of Oceanography, UCSD
8602 La Jolla Shores Drive, La Jolla

Media check in at *Surf Bowl Central* (follow signs to *Surf Bowl Central* from La Jolla Shores Drive).

BACKGROUND: The NOSB is an educational program and competition developed to increase students' knowledge and understanding of the oceans. The program also raises the visibility of ocean-related research, and emphasizes the importance of ocean conservation.

TEAMS: La Jolla High School (La Jolla), Montgomery High School, Francis Parker High School (San Diego), John Muir Alternative School (San Diego), Multi Media Visual Arts School at Crawford Complex (San Diego), San Clemente High School (San Clemente), Charter School of San Diego (San Diego), Sage Hill High School (Newport Beach), Mar Vista High School (San Diego), University City High School (San Diego), Carlsbad High School (Carlsbad), Buckeye Union High School (Arizona), Christian High School (San Diego), Salpointe Catholic High School (Arizona), Scripps Ranch High School (Scripps Ranch), and Preuss School of Science Connections and Technology at Kearny High Complex (San Diego)

-more-

SCRIPPS COMMUNICATIONS
9500 Gilman Drive, Dept 0233 • La Jolla, California • 92093-0233 • Tel: (858) 534-3624 • Fax: (858) 534-5306
Web: aquarium.ucsd.edu • scrippsnews.ucsd.edu • E-mail: scrippsnews@ucsd.edu

EARTHQUAKE! Life on a Restless Planet Exhibit Has *Rumbled* in

Secrets of the Seahorse

EXHIBIT HONORED WITH PRESTIGIOUS AWARD

The American Zoo and Aquarium Association (AZA) and The Curtis and Edith Munson Foundation have honored Birch Aquarium at Scripps with the eighth annual Munson Aquatic Conservation Exhibitry (M.A.C.E.) Award for our *Secrets of the Seahorse* exhibit. The award was announced at a special presentation during AZA's recent 80th annual conference.

Secrets of the Seahorse is a 2,000-square foot interactive exhibition that showcases 13 species of live animals native both to local waters and abroad, ranging from the endangered Knysna seahorse from South Africa to the largest seahorse species, the local

Why is a seahorse a fish?
Interactive exhibit on seahorse anatomy

Pacific seahorse. Through engaging and thought-provoking hands-on displays, the exhibit illustrates why seahorses are actually fish, how male seahorses become pregnant and give birth, and many other amazing seahorse truths. *Secrets of the Seahorse* also features a seahorse breeding laboratory where visitors can observe the breeding, birthing, feeding, and day-to-day lives of these mysterious fish.

EXPLORE SECRETS OF THE SEAHORSE BEFORE APRIL 17

Since the exhibit's debut in May 2002, more than one million people have explored the unique adaptations and biology of seahorses and their relatives, while learning about the current threats to their survival, and ways to conserve this diminishing creature. After three years, *Secrets of the Seahorse's* last day is April 17. We are creating our newest exhibition, *The Art of Deception*, that will showcase the unique ways sea creatures employ deceptive disguise to aid in their survival.

Birch Aquarium at Scripps will continue to display seahorses and their relatives. In fact, Birch Aquarium received an AZA Bean Award in 1999 recognizing our husbandry department for their work in breeding seahorses in-house and sharing them with international zoos and aquariums in an effort to reduce collecting pressures on natural populations. These seahorse breeding and outreach efforts will continue.

The M.A.C.E. Award was designed to recognize excellence in aquatic exhibits that incorporate conservation education into their design and presentation. The award is given annually in the form of a grant to the winning institution's education department.

Birch Aquarium at Scripps is accredited by the American Zoo and Aquarium Association representing the top 10% of the nation's zoos and aquariums. AZA-accredited organizations are committed to providing excellent care for animals, a great experience for visitors, and a better future for all living things.

We at Birch Aquarium encourage you to visit *Secrets of the Seahorse* again before we bid adieu to this award-winning exhibition.

FACT SHEETS

Fact sheets are exactly what the name suggests—a sheet of facts, void of commentary and editorializing. Fact sheets typically run one to two pages in length. They present the essential facts about a company, an organization, a product or service. They are used with the media, customers and potential customers, and the general public. In fact, they're appropriate for anyone seeking general information.

In the case of a company, organization or institution, a fact sheet would include such information as its name, its stock ticker symbol (if a listed company) and where it's traded, its principal products or services, executive officers, plant or office locations, its sales and profits, its number of employees, and any other basic information deemed pertinent.

Fact sheets are also done for specific products and services. For instance, one could cover the basic facts about a new automobile or hand-held computer, or a new service that helps airline passengers find the best fares.

Fact sheets are simple to write; in fact writing isn't even necessary. All it requires is a listing of the facts.

Fact sheets should be distributed to, and be on file with, key media and updated as necessary.

The following Chevron/Texaco fact sheet illustrates how a major multinational corporation structures its information in a concise, easily assimilated and impressive format. The style used can apply to almost any fact sheet.

ChevronTexaco

Fact Sheet

Global Snapshot

- Fifth largest integrated energy company in the world and second largest in the U.S., based on market capitalization, as of Dec. 31, 2003
- Active in more than 180 countries
- Employees: approximately 47,000 people worldwide (excluding service station employees, as of Nov. 30, 2004)
- Capital and exploratory spending budget (2004): $8.5 billion, as of Dec. 31, 2003

Financial Highlights

- Sales and other operating revenues – $120.0 billion
- Net income – $7.2 billion; $6.96 per share – diluted
- Return on average capital employed – 15.7%
- Return on average stockholders' equity – 21.3%
- Cash dividends – $2.86 per share
- Total stockholder return – 35.2%

As of Dec. 31, 2003

Accomplishments

Global Upstream – Exploration and Production

- **Crude oil and natural gas reserves** – Addition of 1 billion net oil-equivalent barrels; equal to 108 percent of 2003 production; 11th consecutive year reserve additions exceeded annual production.
- **Crude oil and natural gas production** – 2.5 million net oil-equivalent barrels per day.
- **Exploration** – Deepwater discoveries in the Gulf of Mexico at Saint Malo, Tubular Bells, Perseus and Sturgis, and in Nigeria at Nsiko; successful appraisal drilling for earlier discoveries at Tahiti and Great White in Gulf of Mexico, Io-Jansz offshore Australia, and Aparo and Usan in Nigeria.
- **Major project start-ups** – Production from Chad crude oil fields transported by pipeline to coast of Cameroon for export; integrated operation of the mine and upgrader at the Athabasca Oil Sands Project in western Canada.

Global Gas

- **North America** – Deepwater port license for construction of Port Pelican liquefied natural gas (LNG) terminal offshore Louisiana; filing of permits for construction of LNG terminal offshore Baja California, Mexico, to supply North American market.
- **Australia** – Approval in principle for Gorgon Joint Venture's construction of natural gas processing facility on Barrow Island; agreement with China National Offshore Oil Corporation to negotiate purchase of Gorgon gas and acquisition of ownership equity in the Gorgon project.
- **Nigeria** – Agreement with partners to advance plans to conduct front-end engineering and design for a new LNG facility at Brass River.

Global Downstream – Refining, Marketing and Transportation

- **Worldwide reorganization** – Realignment of businesses along global functional lines from previous geographic orientation; objective is to improve operating efficiencies and overall financial performance.
- **Clean fuels** – Completion of projects at refineries in Pascagoula, Mississippi; Pembroke, United Kingdom; and Rotterdam, Netherlands, to increase yields and enable the manufacture of low-sulfur fuels.

Chemicals

- **New manufacturing facilities** – Commissioning by 50 percent-owned Chevron Phillips Chemical Company LLC of world-scale polyolefins complex in Qatar and high-density polyethylene plant at Cedar Bayou, Texas.

Corporate Objectives

- **Achieve sustained financial returns** that will enable ChevronTexaco to outperform its competitors.
- **Generate the highest total stockholder return** among a designated peer group of the 3 largest competitors for the 5-year period 2000–2004; the company had the highest return among the peer group for the 2000–2003 period.

Updated: December 2004

ChevronTexaco

ChevronTexaco Headquarters
6001 Bollinger Canyon Road
San Ramon, CA 94583
www.chevrontexaco.com
+1 925 842 0050

INTERACTIVE EXERCISES CHAPTER 12

Media Kits and Fact Sheets

Exercise One

Contact media outlets or companies or your university and obtain a media kit. Assess the media kit, looking at design and content. In your opinion, how effective is the cover in setting the tone or creating interest? How useful would the kit be to a broadcast medium? How is the information packaged for use by radio? Television? Newspapers?

Exercise Two

List important considerations in creating a media kit for a 50th anniversary of a company, organization or institution. Describe or create a cover and list the contents you would want to include in the kit.

Exercise Three

In addition to distributing the kits to the media, what other audiences might find them useful? Write a paragraph explaining the other targets for the kits that might be tailored for distribution beyond the media.

Use the CD-ROM to compare your work with our suggestions.

## CHAPTER THIRTEEN

WRITING FOR RADIO AND TV: NEWS, FEATURES AND PSAs

Consumers in developed countries live in an electronic community. So it comes as no surprise that most people report they get the bulk of their news and information from the electronic media. Radio and television, and to a lesser degree, but increasingly, the Internet, are said to be the principal sources of news and information. In conjunction with movies, these forces are considered to be arbiters of what is acceptable and desirable and hence shape perceptions about everything from products to presidential candidates.

Since the influence of the electronic media, particularly radio and television, is mighty, it is important to explore how writing for radio and television is different from writing for print.

These are the key differences:

- When writing for print, your target is the *reader*
- When writing for radio, your target is the *listener*
- When writing for television, you are targeting *both the listener and the viewer*

For both radio and television, the mission is: *keep it short and keep it simple.*

THE BASICS STAY THE SAME

The same principles that apply to writing for print apply to writing for the electronic media:

- a lead that grabs attention,
- the Five Ws formula for determining content, and
- the inverted pyramid construction.

The major difference between print and broadcast media is that the latter will likely reduce your story to nothing more than the lead. Print media deal in column inches, while broadcast media deal in time.

A minute in broadcast, for both radio and television, is an eternity. Try it. Look at your watch, locate the second-hand, and then close your eyes for what you think is one minute. Don't cheat by counting "one-thousand-one, one-thousand-two" under your breath. Just sit there and imagine a minute. Then open your eyes and check the second-hand again. Odds are, unless you are very unusual, you will have lasted about 25 to 40 seconds.

A one-minute story in broadcast is epic. More typical are 10- to 30-second stories. Thus, you have to be able to get the important parts of your story across in that time frame. Ten seconds is equivalent to about 30 words of copy.

This constrained content framework underscores the absolute importance of the writing. Unless you grab and hold your listener right away, the chances are fairly slim that you will get him or her at all.

A PREMIUM ON HOOKS

But, don't put the cart in front of the horse. Unless you successfully grab and hold the interest of the news director, the gatekeeper for what gets aired and what does not, your story won't make it on the air.

As a result, there is a real premium on "hooks" in writing for broadcast. "Hooks" are the elements of the story that grab attention and hold interest, that which engages the listener and/or viewer.

It is also worth noting that writing for broadcast involves a particular challenge not common to print: attention. When reading, an individual's full attention is usually concentrated on what is before him or her. In the case of broadcast, the receiver's attention may be anything but focused. The radio story may be competing with outside noises, background conversations, or wandering minds flitting from work issues to the idiot driver in the next lane. With television, competing for the viewer's attention are the unfinished magazines, trips to the refrigerator, children, channel surfing, etc. Not only do these factors make the task of getting and holding attention difficult, they complicate the process of conveying information. Too frequently what is broadcast is misheard, only slightly heard, misunderstood, or simply missed.

This fact argues further for simplicity and brevity.

Remember that unlike the reader of a print story, the receiver of the broadcast story can't go back to review the details. If he or she does not get it the first time, the story is gone. We've lost one opportunity to share our message. Special care is needed in writing for radio and television—a fact that has given rise to the KISS rule, a cardinal rule of writing for broadcast.

GENERAL RULES OF WRITING FOR BROADCAST

The other cardinal rules of writing for broadcast are:

- Concentrate on finding a "hook" that will grab and hold attention.
- Shift your writing focus from phrasing that is meant to be read to phrasing that is meant to be heard.
- Make it conversational.
- Use the present tense.
- Avoid technical words and jargon.
- Use personal pronouns sparingly (he, she, they) to avoid confusion. The same goes for words like latter and former, etc. Remember, the listener can't go back to check.
- Use verbs as often as possible, adjectives as little as possible.

THE RADIO RELEASE

For radio, write the lead as a teaser. In other words, make the first line provocative and interesting enough, so the receiver wants to know more. Test it by reading it aloud, a strategy fondly known as the old "details at eleven" test (e.g., "Sky Falls! Details at Eleven!").

The next four lines should tell the story, but keep the total length inside 30 seconds. Make it easy for the newscaster to read by phonetically spelling difficult to pronounce names and spelling out numbers (i.e., "QUE-sick" in place of "Cusick" and "one billion" rather than "1,000,000,000").

To give the news director flexibility to make the story larger, or to expand or highlight a particular feature of the story, list on a separate sheet the names and brief credentials of experts or personalities available for on-air comment or interview.

Here is an example of a radio news release taken from a newspaper release which you have seen previously. Take particular note of the information at the end of the release on an expert who will be available for a live interview.

Special To:
San Francisco Bay Area Radio News Directors

FOR IMMEDIATE RELEASE
MONDAY, JANUARY 9, 2005

New Program Will Ease Critical Shortage of Nurses in Bay Area
San Francisco—By this time next year there may be almost enough nurses to go around.

The Gordon & Betty Moore Foundation announced today it will put $110 million into a special program designed to train and qualify nurses to help meet the critical shortage of nurses in San Francisco Bay Area Hospitals, a shortage growing worse year by year as training programs shrink and expenses increase. "This effort won't correct the shortage overnight, but it will make a difference right away, and within several years, we may find no one is being shorted on nursing care," said E. L. Donavan, chief administrator of Mercy Hospital.

The Gordon & Betty Moore Foundation was founded and funded by Gordon Moore, the retired co-founder of Intel. A special part of its approximately $5 billion asset portfolio is focused exclusively on Bay Area needs.

# # #

Attention News Directors:
Jean Delray, administrator of the nursing program grant, is available for interview on short notice this afternoon (12:30 through 6:00 p.m.) and tomorrow morning (8:00 a.m. though 12:00 p.m.)

For additional details, follow-up information, and arrangements for interview time with Ms. Delray, please call or email Mary Aimes, The Gordon & Betty Moore Foundation, cell phone 415-765-8396, maryaimes@moore.org.

THE TELEVISION RELEASE

What appeals to the eye makes all the difference here, so cast your story visually.

Again, write your lead as a teaser. Try to keep it to one or two short sentences deliverable in five to seven seconds.

Unfold the rest of the story in descending order of importance. This the same format as for radio, except you will add a special sheet highlighting the visuals. That sheet will describe the video possibilities that can draw the viewer to the story and keep his attention. The story line and visuals must be compelling enough to convince the news director that airing the story will be worth the station's time and resources.

No matter how good your idea and visuals, you still need to tell the story in no more than 30 seconds.

Just as in radio copy, spell out the hard to pronounce words and the difficult to grasp large numbers.

The television news release on the nursing program story doesn't vary materially from the radio release, except for information on visual possibilities that make the story more appealing.

Special To:

San Francisco Bay Area TV Assignment Editors

FOR IMMEDIATE RELEASE
MONDAY, JANUARY 9, 2005

Help is on the Way: New Program Will Ease Critical Shortage of Nurses in Bay Area
San Francisco, CA—By this time next year there may be almost enough nurses to go around.

The Gordon & Betty Moore Foundation announced today it will put $110 million into a special program designed to train and qualify nurses to help meet the critical shortage of nurses in San Francisco Bay Area Hospitals, a shortage growing worse year by year as training programs shrink and expenses increase. "This effort won't correct the shortage overnight, but it will make a difference right away, and within several years, we may find no one is being shorted on nursing care," said E. L. Donavan, chief administrator of Mercy Hospital.

The Gordon & Betty Moore Foundation was founded and funded by Gordon Moore, the retired co-founder of Intel. A special part of its approximately $5 billion asset portfolio is focused exclusively on Bay Area needs.

# # #

Attention Assignment Editors:
Jean Diaz, administrator of the nursing program grant will be available for interviews at our Presidio Headquarters this afternoon (12:30 to 6:00 p.m.) and tomorrow (8:00 a.m. to 2 p.m.) She is fully informed on the details of the program, can speak to the nursing crisis locally and

nationally, and is an articulate interview subject who makes difficult information easily understandable.

Visual possibilities are strong, from the high tech accoutrements of the Foundation Offices to its setting in the Presidio in Golden Gate Park. Additionally, Children's Hospital in Oakland and Mercy Hospital in San Francisco and their head nurses have agreed to make themselves available for location shots and/or interviews.

For arrangements, please contact: Mary Aimes, The Gordon & Betty Moore Foundation, cell phone 415-765-8396; email maryaimes@moore.org.

VNRs AND OTHER PACKAGES

The process discussed above applies to stories that fall in the general category defined earlier as news. The stories are timely, because an announcement is being made, an action of some sort is being taken, or one will be taken soon. You expect the station to staff these sorts of stories—to take your release, rework it, supplement it with interview sound-bites, insert the appropriate video footage to illustrate the story, and have it read on-air by an on-staff newscaster.

There are occasions when immediacy is not a consideration, when you seek a special effect, or when you hope to have total control of what is seen and said. In those instances, a full package is provided to both radio and television in the form of a pre-produced segment. For television, these segments are called Video News Releases (VNRs). A VNR is packaged one of two ways: as a complete story in words and pictures on videotape, to include narration, or with the visual story on tape sans narration. In this case, a print version of the narration copy is provided for the station personality to read on air. VNRs, though effective tools, are not inexpensive and are usually put together by commercial services. These service agencies handle all aspects of VNR production, to include distribution. Similarly, audio releases are sometimes produced and provided to radio stations.

TALK SHOWS AND MAGAZINE FORMATS

Outside the news arena, there is another universe made up of talk show and magazine format programs. These programs have a voracious appetite and are fertile ground for features of a particular type. Producers are almost always looking for provocative and/or offbeat subjects, or at the very least, subjects of high current interest or significance. While there are opportunities on shows of this type, there are also hazards. The positive and negative benefits should be weighed very carefully, prior to committing to such a show.

Winning a placement requires a considerably more aggressive approach than sending out a release. Typically, a "pitch" is needed to sell the idea. This is much like a "pitch" constructed for a print editor to sell a story idea for an article (refer to the chapter on selling story ideas). The pitch goes directly to the producer, by name, of the show you are targeting and can be made through a proposal delivered by phone, FAX, e-mail or messenger. Don't waste your time, or hers, unless: (1) you have a compelling idea which fits the show's style and audience, (2) you can present it convincingly, and (3) its use will materially advance your objectives.

THE 10-SECOND SOUND-BITE

A very important aspect of writing for broadcast is the 10-second sound-bite. These are talking points that are intended to be presented verbally by a spokesman in a live or taped interview. They make your key points succinctly and convincingly. These are carefully written phrases that compress the essence of your message into a concise and memorable line. They are almost like slogans, in that they're short, arresting, and easily understandable. This is very demanding writing. Writing tight, or concisely, is always more difficult than writing loose. The outcome warrants the effort, however. These short messages give your client the focus, and often the eloquence, to make sure your important points are registered with impact and clarity.

How do you write them?

1. List what you think to be the five or six most important points to be made. What are the absolute, bottom-line points your constituents need to know?
2. Ask one or two colleagues or subject matter experts whose opinions you value if they agree on the most important points.
3. Discuss how they would phrase the same points.
4. Synthesize and cull what you think are the best ideas, and phrase the points in straight declarative sentences.
5. Walk around the block, visit someone else's office, get a cup of coffee, or find another way to get away from the process briefly.
6. Then return, pick up what you have written, and rework your draft into the strongest, clearest, most memorable single-sentence, slogan-like phrases you can fashion. These will be your key messages.

The classic example of a memorable sound bite is President John F. Kennedy's description of the goal of the United States space program, which was ". . . to put a man on the moon in this decade." Perfect.

The sound-bite technique also works well in almost any circumstance—with employees, customers, shareholders, etc. Being able to get across important messages in 10 seconds or so is an invaluable asset in a fast-moving and message-cluttered world.

PSAs

Commercial broadcasters, local radio and television stations, and traditional broadcast networks and cable networks, are required to devote a certain portion of their broadcast time each day to air messages deemed to be in the public interest. This is in exchange for the broadcasters' free use of "the public airways" to make a profit.

This public service time is made available to various not-for-profit organizations and causes without charge.

For the most part, the time made available consists of 30-second to one-minute messages called "Public Service Announcements," which generally air at odd hours of the day, night or early morning. Audiences at these times are likely to be small. Even so, PSAs provide an exposure and reach quite valuable to not-for-profits.

Radio PSAs are put together no differently than a good 30-second commercial spot. They start with an arresting hook to attract the listener, followed by a concise voicing of the selling message (e.g., "Give your junker car to the Society for the Something Or Other," or, "Smart kids don't do drugs.").

Radio PSAs are usually provided as self-contained audio-tape or CD-ROM packages that can be shoved into a player and run when scheduled. Sometimes just a script is forwarded to be read and produced by station staff.

Television PSAs normally take the form of a fully-produced 30-second taped announcement, with strong visuals and professional production values, to include sound, lighting, pacing, content and voice. They need to be every bit as good as the run of spots produced by professionals for the station's advertisers. The epitome of television PSAs is the series produced by the Ad Council for the various causes it supports. These are superb. Few, if any, not-for-profits can afford to match these efforts.

Organizations that use television PSAs usually hire a professional production company to write, produce, and place them. Amateurs don't fare well at this game. The same thought applies to radio PSAs. If you feel compelled to try to produce either, concentrate on how broadcast commercials are written. The formula is generally:

- A very strong hook,
- A statement of the benefits,
- Then ask for the order. "Asking for the order" requires that you always present an action step you want audience members to take. It can be as simple as understanding the information you've given, or being sympathetic to your point-of-view on the issue you've discussed, or taking action and doing a specific thing.

The following is an example of how one organization went about structuring a 30-second PSA with a scripted commercial meant to be read by a station announcer. Note the format and that the PSA is pitched to a specific time period and event.

UNIVERSITY OF CALIFORNIA, SAN DIEGO

SCRIPPS INSTITUTION OF OCEANOGRAPHY

BIRCH AQUARIUM AT SCRIPPS **N E W S**

<u>CONTACT</u>: Jessica Demian
or Cindy Clark
858/534-3624

Something **Big** is Surfacing!

START: December 20, 2004
STOP: March 30, 2005

<u>:30 Public Service Spot</u>:

Birch Aquarium at Scripps Whale Watching Cruises
Scripps Institution of Oceanography/UCSD

THAR SHE BLOWS…The Birch Aquarium at Scripps Institution of Oceanography is sponsoring exciting cruises to watch migrating gray whales off the coast of San Diego. Every day from December 26 through March 31, you can join a naturalist from the aquarium for a true adventure on the high seas. Catch a rare glimpse of gray whales along their route to the warm breeding and calving waters of Baja California in Mexico. For more information on times, prices, and reservations, call San Diego Harbor Excursion at 6-1-9-2-3-4-4-1-1-1 and request an aquarium cruise.

#   #   #

The Birch Aquarium at Scripps greatly appreciates the airing of this public service announcement as often as possible through March 30, 2005. Thank you!

UCSD

SCRIPPS COMMUNICATIONS
9500 Gilman Drive, Dept 0233 • La Jolla, California • 92093-0233 • Tel: (858) 534-3624 • Fax: (858) 534-5306
Web: aquarium.ucsd.edu • scrippsnews.ucsd.edu • E-mail: scrippsnews@ucsd.edu

This sort of writing isn't like news writing, or even feature writing. This is copy writing for a PSA, similar to a commercial writing, and the skills don't necessarily transfer. If in a do-it-yourself mode, check with your target radio and television stations and ask for their preferences in formatting and running time.

In all these instances remember: keep it short, keep it simple, and always find a hook.

INTERACTIVE EXERCISES CHAPTER 13

Writing for Radio and TV

Exercise One
Using these notes, create a news release for radio:

The Safe Home Project is a non-sectarian home for battered women and children located in San Antonio. It can care for as many as 30 "guests" weekly, with stays usually averaging eight weeks. It is currently turning away approximately ten applicants a week for lack of space. A fund-raising benefit banquet is planned. The proceeds from the dinner will be used to add a four-room addition to the 16-room, three-story 1920s Safe Home house, and to repair a leaking roof, failing plumbing, and a blown-out furnace. Safe Home receives some funding from United Way and has several corporate and individual donors, but its budget is always strained. It cannot possibly fund the badly needed repairs and expansion without major additional new funding, which the staff hopes to raise through the dinner. Elizabeth Dole, former head of the American Red Cross, will be the featured speaker. The San Antonio Wind Symphony Orchestra will perform a short program. The dinner will be held (you pick the date) at (you pick the spot) in San Antonio.

Exercise Two
From the same information, list three suggestions you would submit to television news directors as possible visuals for the story.

Use the CD-ROM to check your responses.

## CHAPTER FOURTEEN

POSITION PAPERS AND FORMAL STATEMENTS

This is where we begin to up the ante, where we really get into the business of trying to explain and persuade. Among the principal instruments for this are position papers and formal statements. Position papers are needed when there is a significant issue or problem, or in rare cases an opportunity, to be managed.

Formal statements are tools used in situations for which a news release isn't advisable. This includes those times you don't want to run the risk of making someone available for comment or interview, but yet still need to get something said in a precise way without elaboration. Such situations usually arise when something sensitive, delicate, controversial or otherwise loaded is in the news or about to become news.

In both cases, you need to be at your very best in helping people understand the situation and appreciate the good and proper reasons for your actions.

To accomplish this, a treasured piece of conventional wisdom needs to be jettisoned: "If they only understood us better, they'd love us more. If they only understood what we are trying to achieve, they would be for us." It is true that understanding can sometimes lead to support, and it is also true that without understanding, it is impossible to build acceptance. But understanding is neither a panacea nor a solution. Understanding, in fact, can prove an unexpected hazard.

Quite often people understand what you are up to perfectly well. They comprehend your reasons very clearly. They fully grasp what you are trying to achieve. They just don't like it. They don't want anything to do with it. They are against it, regardless of the logic of your argument or the eloquence of its presentation.

Understanding doesn't get you where you need to be.

What gets you where you need to be is the recognition on the part of your constituents of *why* they should be for and with you.

POSITION PAPERS

We write position papers to define where we stand on a matter of importance and to generate support for our position. Position papers generally have limited distribution, but the constituencies to whom they are directed are enormously important.

Position papers are intended for those outside our organization whose actions and opinions can help or hurt us and for our own people, so they understand and can explain our position, if necessary.

There is argument from time to time about whether organizations should take positions on matters not directly related to their bottom-line. There is a concern that shareholder money may be wasted and management attention diverted by adventures into issues and areas best left to politicians and activists. There is concern also that with the money and muscle businesses can marshal, they ought not to be allowed to intrude into such issues, because they can pervert and inappropriately influence the outcome.

The counter argument is that institutions have every right to be involved with any matter that affects them, and in the case of business enterprises, with any issue that can have an impact on their profitability. Indeed, they have a responsibility to do so.

The argument expands to suggest that anything that affects the safety, health or quality of life of an organization's stakeholders falls into this category. The reasoning is that anything that impinges on the welfare of stakeholders affects the organization overall. Stakeholders are those with a "stake," direct or indirect, in the organization's success, such as employees, shareholders, customers, suppliers, residents of the cities and states in which the company operates.

Take the case of the Iowa Seed Company (ISC). Hold on to these facts. The Iowa Seed Company's public relations challenges will come up again later in this text.

ISC is a family-owned firm that has been in business for 50 years and has always been managed by a family member. George Owsley, 54, is the current president, following in the footsteps of his father and grandfather. The company is one of two leading providers of seed for corn, wheat, cotton and soybean crops in Iowa. It also supplies fertilizers and pesticides, which it purchases from Monsanto and Dupont. ISC needs to expand in order to remain profitable and competitive. It has chosen Texas and Oklahoma as the mostly likely markets for success. Well-entrenched competition exists in both states, but ISC feels its competitive edge is its highly efficient seed production methods, which gives it a cost advantage. It also provides a type of personalized service which features on-the-spot advice to farmers on the best seeding, fertilizing and pesticides practices. These practices are tailored specifically to the farmer's situation. Nothing similar exists in Texas or Oklahoma.

ISC employs 700 people in Iowa, the majority in the Ames area where 80 percent of the company's seed production is based. Other employees are located in field offices and distribution centers in Algona in the north, Denison in the west, and Centerville in the south. The company expects to create 400 new jobs with the expansion—225 in Texas and 175 in Oklahoma. No jobs will be lost in Iowa, although some key personnel will be relocated to the new states to help with start-up.

If you are ISC, on what issues might you legitimately be expected to take a position? Remember that anything that can affect the company's operations, its ability to operate profitably and/or the welfare of the company's stakeholders is a matter legitimately within the company's sphere of concern.

Using this criterion, ISC could reasonably be expected to take a position on:

- Day Care centers;
- The minimum wage;
- Affordable housing;
- Sales taxes on consumer products;
- Political contributions;
- Education initiatives;

- Equal employment opportunity;
- Responsibility for the clean-up of chemically contaminated sites;
- Gross vehicular weights of trucks allowed on state highways;
- Genetically engineered crops.

All of these issues can and do affect the well being of ISC and its stakeholders.

A Foundation of Facts

To be effective, position papers must be built on facts and offer a clear statement of the reasons behind the position. They must explain why these reasons are sound and responsible. They must either directly or indirectly associate the reader's interests with the position being advanced. And, if the arguments are to have a chance of persuading, they must be reasonable, logical and believable.

The facts must be thoroughly researched and vetted by subject matter experts.

They must then be organized and packaged in compelling, articulate and understandable language. Finding the right tone for this is crucial. If the voice comes across as pontifical or preachy, defensive or whiny, arrogant, presumptuous or imploring, it will alienate the target audience. If the voice seems anything other than reasoned, authoritative, responsible and believable, the arguments it advances simply will not find favor.

As important as voice is inoculating your audience against the arguments of your opponents. Not only must your reasoning be compelling, but the arguments against your position must be thoroughly understood and effectively countered. You may or may not choose to directly address the opposition's claims in your paper. Regardless, your arguments must effectively trump those of the naysayers.

Position papers run from several hundred words to lengthy documents. As in most things, brevity is more effective than verbosity, but also as in most things, it depends on the issue.

For the most part, position papers are used with:

- Government officials at the local, state, federal and international levels, with particular attention to elected individuals and their staffs;
- Key business contacts;
- Key academics;
- Key think-tank personnel;
- Important shareholders and investors;
- Opinion leaders in the communities and special interest areas important to you;
- Key editors and writers;
- Employees, and
- Key and potential customers.

A Template for Writing Position Papers

As with any other writing form, there is a structure for writing position papers. To follow is a bare-bones formula that works well:

- Start with a statement of the issue or problem, framing it as fairly as you can manage. If you skew this, you'll lose credibility immediately.
- Move into a brief statement of the present or expected consequences, both positive and negative.
- Next present your case, emphasizing the reasonable, logical and appropriate reasons why you take this position. Argue persuasively. Find ways to tie your objectives to the interests of the receivers. Structure the order in which you present the facts so that they lead logically to the reasonable conclusion you want people to adopt.
- Summarize and end with a strong statement of the action or conclusion justified by the argument you have presented.

This is only one of many approaches. The key is to pick the approach that packages your argument through compelling logic and persuasive phrases.

Regardless of the way you choose to structure the argument, make sure you pay particular attention to the way you state the issue. If you get to state the issue, you get to define it. If you get to define it, you are in a position that allows you to shape the perception of the matter in the reader's mind. You must state the issue fairly, giving due recognition to the opposing side and projecting objectivity. Still, if you get to define it, you get to pick the ground on which the matter is contested. In military theory, being able to pick the battleground is a major advantage.

Following is an example of a position paper that addresses a current concern of high importance to a particular group. It was intended not only to raise the level of attention to this issue, but to elevate the level of the national debate. The paper was circulated to members of the U.S. Congress, members of state legislatures, key media, and selected clerics and academics.

A MATTER OF FAIRNESS

A Paper on the Need to Protect and Preserve Benefits Earned by Retirees

(This paper was prepared by Kaiser Aluminum Salaried Retirees Association, which represents some 4,500 retirees and surviving spouses throughout the United States. Address: Kaiser Aluminum Salaried Retirees Association, P.O. Box 1171, Lafayette, CA 94549. Phone/fax: 925/284-7009.)

The Issue: Shortchanging Earned Rights

Utilizing the legal system and, in particular, the corporate bankruptcy process, Corporate America increasingly is shortchanging the rights of retirees. The injustice and resulting hardship are spreading like a virus. Company after company, either as a part of bankruptcy reorganization or simply as a way to reduce costs, is reneging on providing the medical, insurance, and other benefits that retirees earned while on the job.

Forgotten are the contributions these former employees made during their careers to the viability of their companies.

Overlooked is the fact that, unlike active employees, retirees cannot make up lost benefits by moving to another employer. Instead, retirees are the victims of broken promises and a legal system and bankruptcy process that ignores their claims while recognizing those of bondholders, creditors, and other constituents.

Corporations routinely label retiree benefits as "legacy costs" as if they belong to a business that has faded into history and are no longer an obligation. Or, they regard them as an obligation that is expendable when and if the going gets a bit tough. This is wrong. Retiree benefits are *earned* benefits. . . not bequeathed. . . but *earned* by each generation of employees through valuable work done and real services rendered in helping companies reach their performance goals. They are as much an obligation of any publicly chartered business as any obligation it holds. And, if companies and "the system" don't recognize this, they should.

It all boils down to a matter of fairness. Throughout America's history—whether the issue was voting rights, educational opportunity, or access to employment—we as a society have sought to make fair that which was not. When a part of our system was broken, we found a way to fix it.

That is what is needed now to protect and preserve the benefits that retirees earned during their employment. Unless the system is fixed, a large part of America's fastest growing population segment will suffer unfair and unnecessary economic hardship.

Background: Broken Promises

Medical and insurance benefits have long been a sizeable part of the total compensation package larger and many smaller companies have provided their employees. Companies have used the attractiveness of their benefits programs as a selling point to recruit and retain employees. In some cases, companies avoided spending a portion of their profits for salary increases and, instead, promised retirement benefits.

For employees, a major part of the attraction has been that the benefits will be there for them to use in their retirement years when medical needs predictably increase.

Traditionally, the companies providing these benefits have borne the full cost except for affordable deductibles and relatively nominal co-payments for visits to doctors' offices and for prescription drugs. As employees of these companies have retired and become eligible for Medicare, they have had the assurance that their retiree medical benefit program would be there to cover prescription drugs and medical services not covered by Medicare.

That expectation, that assurance is now changing. An increasing number of companies are transferring to retirees more and more of the costs of providing such benefits. The amounts transferred constitute, at the least, an unforeseen burden and, at the worst, an unaffordable expense. Other companies are canceling outright the medical benefits retirees had earned.

No one doubts that the cost of providing medical benefits increases each year—as service providers increase their rates and as the number of retirees increases. No one denies the need for companies to be as competitive as they can be, and to reduce costs wherever possible and appropriate. However, benefits programs constitute promises made—promises that should be kept.

One Approach to Solving the Problem: No After-the-Fact Reductions

One approach to solving the problem is contained in a bill (H.R. 1322) authored in 2001 and reintroduced in March 2003 by Congressman John Tierney (D., MA). This measure would amend the Employee Retirement Income Security Act (ERISA) of 1974 to provide emergency protection for retiree health benefits.

H.R. 1322 states that retirees "have been severely harmed by the virtually unchecked practices of sponsors of (group health plans) involving the post-retirement cancellation or reduction of health benefits which retirees counted on receiving for their lifetimes. Such widespread post-retirement reductions in retiree health benefits have led to a crisis in retiree health care." It further points out that, "In many instances, (retirees) have failed to obtain adequate relief in the courts due to highly restrictive judicial interpretations which are inconsistent with ERISA's underlying protective purposes."

To correct this inequity, H.R. 1322 would:

- Bar the sponsors of medical benefit plans from cancelling or reducing benefits *after* participants retire;
- Require sponsors to restore health benefits previously taken away from participants after they retired, so long as the sponsor would not sustain substantial business hardship by restoring the benefits;
- Establish an Emergency Retiree Health Loan Guarantee Program to assist sponsors of group health plans obligated to restore benefits to obtain Federally guaranteed loans to do so.

The scope of H.R. 1322 is broad and clear: "Notwithstanding that a group health plan may contain a provision reserving the general power to amend or terminate the plan or a provision specifically authorizing the plan to make post-retirement reductions in retiree health benefits, it shall be prohibited for any group health plan. . . to reduce the benefits provided to a retired participant or beneficiary. . . if such reduction of benefits occurs after the date the participant retired. . ."

The bill defines what it means by a prohibited reduction of benefits as (1) cancelling, decreasing or limiting the amount, type, level, or form of any benefit or option provided prior to the amendment of the plan or action; (2) imposing or increasing the out-of-pocket costs a retired participant or beneficiary must pay in order to keep or obtain any benefits that were provided prior to the amendment or action; or (3) modifying the manner by which medical services are delivered under the plan so that a retired participant or beneficiary has less ready access to the delivery of such services than before the amendment or action.

Another Legislative Approach: Inclusion in the Process

Another separate legislative approach—H.R. 975, the Bankruptcy Abuse and Consumer Protection Act—also has merit. Because changes in retiree medical benefits or termination of coverage often occur during the process of a Chapter 11 bankruptcy reorganization, bankruptcy law needs to be changed to ensure that employees and retirees are represented in the bankruptcy process. Currently, with few exceptions, they are not.

The House of Representatives has acted on H.R. 975, adding provisions to accomplish changes in the treatment of some pension obligations in the bankruptcy process. However, the House provisions are quite limited and apply only to bankruptcy proceedings that are initiated in the future—not to those which are currently in bankruptcy court and have not yet presented or received court approval for a plan of reorganization.

The Senate needs to improve H.R. 975, so that it provides better representation of retirees as creditors and increased security for retiree benefits in current as well as future bankruptcy proceedings. Specifically, H.R. 975 needs to be amended to include provisions that would:

- Assure that the Bankruptcy Code protects, to the greatest extent possible, the interests and benefits claims of all retirees; and
- Assure that the court appoints a Special Trustee to oversee retiree benefits and appoints representatives of retirees to serve on an official creditors committee.

Who's Affected?

It seems like each day brings a new bankruptcy. Corporations which for years had been "household names" are now distressed to the point of filing for Chapter 11 bankruptcy protection.

A May 2003 article in The Wall Street Journal noted that, in the steel industry alone, more than 30 companies have filed for bankruptcy protection since 1998. The reasons vary but the results—all too often for retirees and their beneficiaries are the same, i.e., medical benefits either are reduced or eliminated.

For well over a decade, in some instances, retirees have found it necessary to form their own associations in an effort to protect and preserve benefits. These company-specific groups have multiplied dramatically in recent years. In 1996, the Coalition for Retirement Security (CRS) was formed as an all-volunteer, national grassroots organization with a mission "to correct inequities affecting workers and retirees whose expected pensions and health insurance coverage have been unfairly diminished or denied." CRS is also "committed to educating policymakers and the American public about the importance of retirement security to the nation's workers." Two years ago, a number of CRS member groups formed a lobbying organization, the National Retirees Legislative Network (NRLN), specifically to focus on securing enactment of H.R. 1322.

The Urgency

AARP reports that some 41 million people have no health insurance. Unless corrective action is taken now, that number will surely increase as employers cut back on coverage for active employees and retirees. In 2001, according to William M. Mercer, an employee benefits firm, only 23 percent of large employers offered medical insurance to retirees, compared with 40 percent in 1993. Similar reductions have been occurring in pension benefit coverage, with employers substituting inadequate savings plans with no protection, or reducing originally promised pension benefits when converting to "cash balance" type plans.

Any politicians doubting the depth of their constituents' concerns on medical costs and coverage need only review a recent poll by the Kaiser Family Foundation. According to AARP, worries about rising health care costs ranked first among 13 issues surveyed by the Foundation.

Nearly 38 percent responded they were "very worried" the cost of their health care services or insurance will increase over the next six months.

Company-provided medical benefits for active employees, retirees and beneficiaries have been a key ingredient in the improved health of our population and the lengthening of life expectancies. They have helped assure that needed medical services both preventative and corrective—are sought and provided. Ways need to be found to perpetuate, strengthen and expand this coverage—not eliminate it. Promises need to be kept, laws need to be changed, and the benefits that retirees earned need to be preserved and protected.

It's all about fairness.

# # #

STATEMENTS

A reporter for the *Houston Chronicle* has picked up rumors about Iowa Seed Company's planned expansion into Texas and Oklahoma. He queries. You know that if the *Chronicle* has picked up the rumor, other Texas media will follow shortly. You're not ready to make the formal announcement. There are still important loose ends to pin down. Yet you want to get off on the right foot with the *Chronicle* and you want to make sure the first media mentions of ISC in Texas are positive. This means you want to be cooperatively responsive.

So you decide to issue a formal statement.

For many companies in this situation, the formal statement would be, "ISC does not respond to rumors." This can be a good position. It's conservative. It protects your options. It commits you to nothing. It is also, in essence, a "no comment" response, which reporters and editors generally take to mean guilty as charged or, "You've got it right, but we aren't going to tell you anything."

"No comment" responses, though fully expected by the media, don't satisfy anyone except the company's attorneys. Their reasoning is that what you don't say can't hurt you. This may be true enough in courtrooms, but in the court of public opinion, what you don't say is often what kills you.

A Controlled Message

Since we've decided we want to be cooperative and get our positive points out in a *controlled manner,* we issue a formal statement. In doing this, we're saying what we have to say, but not running the risk that further elaboration may lead us down paths we don't yet want to tread.

The statement reads:

The Iowa Seed Company, a family-owned and managed firm that has been serving Midwestern agriculture for 40 years, is considering expanding its services to farmers and ranchers in Texas and Oklahoma within the next six to nine months. The Company is a major supplier of seed and other products to the Iowa agricultural economy. Its services are individually tailored to the needs of each of its clients, an approach it believes will allow it to be competitive in new markets and which can bring value to Texas and Oklahoma farmers and ranchers. ISC expects to establish service centers in the Dallas and Houston areas and to bring approximately 150 new jobs into the state, if final marketing studies and site explorations prove successful. Pending this, no additional details are available at present.

Since this is a formal statement, it is written. It is given, either in writing or read word-for-word, to the reporter who came with the initial query and subsequently to all others who inquire. Its purpose is to make it clear that this is all we have to say about the matter at this time, and nothing more.

Since the statement is written, we can also choose to distribute it in the same way we would a release, hitting all media before they've asked the question. We might do this, because we want to gain visibility for the ISC name to support marketing activities that will soon commence. If we distribute the statement to broader audiences, we would headline it: "A Statement from the Iowa Seed Company Regarding Expansion Plans in Texas and Oklahoma."

With the statement, we have been responsive to the media. We've covered the basic information. We, hopefully, have closed the door on further inquiry until we are ready to make a full-scale announcement. Media will keep coming with questions. But we stay with the statement. Period.

As statements go, this one is in the middle of the range for length. Some formal statements are much longer, becoming almost position-paper length. Some are shorter. The idea is to say what you need to say, make your points, and then get out of it. You want to cover as many of the Five Ws in the statement as possible. You want it to sound and be authoritative. And you want to make it clear that this is all that can be said on the matter at the moment.

Formal statements put the organization on record, without revealing more than you are ready to reveal.

BELIEVABILITY

We close this section with a word on believability. If no one believes you, nothing you say will make any difference.

Believability is defined as that which is "capable of eliciting belief or trust . . . seemingly or apparently likely or acceptable."

A thing is "believable" if it tracks with your experience, or with what you've been told by those you trust, or what you understand to be the normal way of things, or if it has been attested to by people whose expertise, experience or accomplishments give them credibility.

To be acceptable, an argument must be believable. To be believable, it must conform to the reader's view of what is likely. Lacking personal experience that tells them otherwise or credible evidence to the contrary, most people are willing to believe almost anything which to them seems reasonable. Never try to argue the unreasonable.

INTERACTIVE EXERCISES CHAPTER 14

Position Papers and Formal Statements

Exercise One

The production and sale of genetically modified seed for food crops is under fire by a committee of the Iowa state legislature, with hearings set to explore whether the product should be banned. ISC grows and sells genetically modified seed for corn, wheat and rice. The company contends that genetically modified seed produces bigger yields per acre than conventional seed, is insect resistant, making the use of pesticides unnecessary, can produce bountiful crops in marginal farming areas where water is in limited supply, and has been sufficiently tested to indicate that resulting food is safe for human consumption.

Opponents say the use of such seed runs the risk of unleashing unknown and unanticipated viruses that can devastate conventional crops and produce new and untreatable sickness in humans. Therefore, they argue, it should be banned until sufficient tests have been run over an extended period of time (20 years) to assess the full impact of the use of genetically altered seed on humans and the environment.

A. Write a one page position paper favoring whichever side of this issue you choose. Use the template in this chapter as a guide.

Exercise Two

Media want to know about rumors that cost over-runs at your local plant may require a layoff of 100 people. A study to determine the necessity and potential scope of lay-offs is nearly complete. Pending the final result of that study, which will almost certainly recommend a lay-off, the plant manager doesn't want to provide information to the media. If a lay-off is in fact necessary, he wants to inform employees first.

A. Write the statement you would use to respond to media inquiries.
B. Would you respond only to the inquiring reporters, or would you distribute the statement for broad public consumption?
C. In this case, would you decline to comment? Briefly explain your decision.

Use the CD-ROM to check your answers.

## CHAPTER FIFTEEN

BRIEFING PAPERS AND Q&As

Arguably the most important writing done for public relations is not intended for the public. It is aimed, rather, at the movers and shakers within your own company or organization. This writing is intended to provide the information and rationale upon which important decisions are made, to set strategy and lay tactics for important actions that are to be taken, or to prepare managers for successful encounters with media or any of the core constituencies that impact the firm's health and prospects.

The purpose of such writing is to accurately describe a situation and lay out a plan for how it is to be handled, by whom and when. When this thinking, analyzing and projecting is boiled down into a document from which a decision can be made, or upon which an action can be based, it is called a *briefing paper.*

The importance of the briefing paper relies more on the excellence of the thinking than the quality of the writing. Yet, the way in which the argument is presented and the skill with which the recommendation is articulated affects its reception and success. The writing must be lucid and convincing; it must make the case that supports the recommendation being made.

WHAT A BRIEFING PAPER SHOULD CONTAIN

The following is a summary of what a briefing paper should do:

1. Present the facts,
2. offer a clear and realistic interpretation of the facts,
3. make recommendations for actions or decisions based on these facts,
4. outline a suggested plan of action, and
5. assess the likely results.

The key to this exercise is to think of everything that might be of any conceivable consequence to the matter and eliminate, as completely as possible, any and all surprises.

Briefing papers fall into two broad categories: policy and action.

Policy briefs are those that outline a rationale and action plan for a decision or a position. Briefing papers of this type usually deal with issues.

An action brief is intended to prepare the recipient for an upcoming event or to recommend that a particular action be taken, again with the necessary supporting material.

If your CEO is scheduled for an interview with a media outlet, you would create a briefing paper that explains what to expect and includes a recommendation on how to handle the situation. The same would be done for the chief marketing manager in preparation for a series of meetings with key customers. You would also prepare this type of brief to help prepare people for speeches, meetings with community leaders, employee sessions, trade conferences or congressional hearings.

CONSTRUCTING A BRIEFING PAPER

An upcoming news conference for the Iowa Seed Company will serve as the example.

The mission is to make sure your principal is prepared and to suggest a course of action that will help produce the best results for the company.

The briefing paper will be directed to the presentation team for the news conference and to the public relations staff members responsible for the event. It will also explain the rationale for the news conference and emphasize the points necessary to supporting ISC's successful entry into the market. The actual event is planned for 11 a.m., Thursday, in the Johnson Room of the Dallas Hilton Hotel.

The briefing paper should cover the following elements:

1. The rationale for holding the event
2. An assessment of all potential positive and negative results
3. Details on where it is to be staged and when
4. The names of the recommended participants from the company and what role they will play
5. The names of the media expected to be present, along with background information on each person. Special reference should be given to those considered most important for your purposes or those who might be a potential problem and why.
6. The ground rules for the session—is it to be on-the-record, or are parts to be off-the-record or background only? (As a matter of policy, news conferences should always be on-the-record). In regard to the ground rules, stipulate how reporters will be recognized (e.g., raised hand, etc.) and whether they will be asked to identify themselves and their organizations.
7. The management aspects of the session:
   A. Identify who will run the session as the "Masters of Ceremonies." Is it the public relations manager or a senior member of the ISC management?
   B. List the order in which each presenter will speak.
   C. Indicate who will close the session, how and when.
8. The message points. Present, in writing, key points that should be made in the session with suggestions on how each should be phrased.
9. Potential Q&As. Include a list of the questions likely to be asked by the assembled media and provide appropriate responses.
10. The remaining logistics of the meeting:
    A. Indicate how the players should be attired (business formal, business casual, or other).
    B. Describe how the room is to be set-up. Will you use a raised podium and if so, how will it be situated relative to the audience? Will the audience be seated theatre-style or at tables?

In regard to sound, will there be a single microphone or multiple? Also provide a sketch of the room, showing the speakers' podium, audience seating area, entry and exit ways and windows.

C. List the takeaways or hand-outs that will be available and when they will be offered (e.g., a hard copy of a release, a media kit, product samples or mementos).

D. Close with a paragraph setting a time, date and location for rehearsing the presenters on the message points and Q&A.

The above, though for a relatively routine event, is a format that can be used for all briefing papers.

To summarize, briefing papers answer two questions: (1) What do my players need to know about the matter, in order to understand and handle it intelligently? and, (2) What is the best advice on what to do and how to do it?

Following is an example of a briefing paper for a meeting to outline the strategy for an important initiative. The paper specifies the basic strategic elements to be considered and provides details for the meeting. Briefing papers are not always brief, but they should always be concise.

BRIEFING NOTES:
For Tuesday, Oct. 30 Meeting
Ad Hoc Benefits Action Committee
Subject: Strategy for National Effort Re: Project Save 'Em

Committee Members:

We have three basic approaches to consider:

1. Continue with the present program but expand it to include action-steps to be taken by association members to raise visibility for the issue with selected influential stakeholders and stimulate their support and/or actions.

2. Launch a coordinated and centrally managed broad scale communications effort designed to draw high public visibility to the impending action, spinning off the fairness issue, and directed at:

    · Influential local and national media (general readership, business, and trade press; television news, talk, and news-magazine shows; radio news and talk shows);

    · Potentially sympathetic Internet chat rooms and bulletin boards;

    · Plant state members of the Congress and their staffs;

    · Members of state legislatures representing districts where our plants are (or have been) operational;

    · Newsletters and other communications devices of potentially sympathetic organizations;

    · Civic and service clubs in cities where plants are (or have been) operational—and in our corporate HQ city;

- Pastors of churches in cities where plants are (or have been) operational—and in the corporate HQ city;
- Officers of chambers of commerce in cities where plants are (or have been) operational—and in the corporate HQ city;
- Well-known national advocates of health care reform, employee and retiree rights, and/or responsible actions by corporations toward all their stakeholders.

3. Launch an aggressive communications program designed to raise questions about the motives of the "newcomer" executive team responsible for the present plight and who will be making the crucial decisions on health and retirement benefits for retirees and present employees . . . the idea being to put a strong enough public spotlight on them that they may be inclined to "do the right thing" or, short of that, adopt a more accommodating negotiating stance.

This last option is a non-starter. It is likely to be more counter-productive than helpful and not consistent with the style or spirit of the corporate culture the leaders and employees of this company grew up in and lived with during their active careers. It is included only for those who had the momentary taste of blood in their mouths.

Though this needs to be debated, Option #2 appears to offer the probability that a high degree of public visibility across a broad range of constituencies could be generated, stimulating useful sympathy, and even support—all of which could be translated into a negotiating advantage.

Part of the idea here is to put present management on notice that if you're going to rape us, you're going to have to do it in the glare of a very strong public spotlight and why not be responsible, reasonable, and cooperative . . . suggesting that "Doing the right thing," may be the best option in the long run.

We need to brainstorm how the fairness argument can be effectively made and what else can be thrown into the mix to "enrich" it.

Clearly, this isn't going to be free. We will need to discuss the amount of budget likely to be needed and decide how to gather the funds.

The meeting is set for 9 a.m., Tuesday, Oct. 30, in the Salisbury Conference Room, second floor. Plan to be there the full day. Lunch will be served. Your undistracted attention is needed for this project, so leave your cell phones off. We'll break at 10:30 a.m., 12:30 p.m. and 3:30 p.m. Your can catch up with your messages during these times.

As we have previously agreed, and as is restated here for emphasis, before anything gets moving, **we need to be in firm agreement as to the *realistic* outcome we expect as a result of this effort**. Otherwise, we're only spinning wheels.

Q&As

Like briefing papers, question and answer sheets (Q&As) are among the most important pieces that public relations writers prepare.

This is because Q&As are most frequently used to help clients prepare and rehearse for important media interviews, shareholder meetings, meetings with key customers and customer groups, or to perform confidently in public or private situations where questions can be expected.

The Q&A should anticipate all substantive questions likely to be asked. This requires some knowledge of the questioner and his or her interests. The Q&A sheet should also provide the best answers for the anticipated questions, phrased in language most likely to be convincing and easily understood.

Pay particular attention to the tough questions that might be asked, so your client can deal with them confidently and with authority

Also pay special attention to the questions you hope your client will be asked, because these allow you to highlight the information you want emphasized. If these questions don't come, provide suggestions on how to bridge from the answer of an unrelated question to the matter you want to discuss. In other words, find a way for your client to include the key messages when answering almost any question (a.k.a. "bridging").

Q&As frequently including a set of "talking points." Talking points cover the key points to be made, regardless of whether the question is asked or the subject is raised.

Good Q&As Are Built on Good Research

Quality Q&As require research. You must go to the people who have the information necessary to answer the questions you anticipate. On occasion you may want to assemble a group to brainstorm possible answers. Sometimes you may go it entirely alone, based on what you already know and how you feel about the way a particular question should be handled. Always, though, be sure that the information is correct.

Think of this as you would were you preparing a client for testimony at a trial. In that sense, your client must be fully prepared for anything and everything. He must be confident, articulate, truthful beyond question, and persuasive overall.

The writer has a huge responsibility, as he or she must not only anticipate what's coming, but recommend the appropriate response.

Depending on the situation, a Q&A sheet might run no longer than one page with only three or four questions. They can, though, run to multiple pages, with a multiplicity of questions and answers. Q&As for shareholder meetings quite frequently run so large they must be put into three-ring binders.

The format for developing a Q&A is simple: state the question and then answer it.

Here is an example of a typical Q&A. This one is designed to prepare a group of three executives for an upcoming newspaper interview that will serve as the basis for a major feature story on their company. Note that it carries information on both the reporter and the intended story. It outlines the basic strategy for the interviews and explains the ground rules.

Talking Points and Q&A for Upcoming *Atlanta Constitution* Interview

The talking points below are meant to set a basic framework, so that all participants have a shared understanding of the material to be covered and suggestions on how the points can be effectively phrased.

Jim, Ed, and Don will carry the basic load in "telling the story." The reporter (Edna Overby) will be here at 9:30 a.m. on Wednesday. She'll be brought to each of your offices in turn for private interview time with each of you (allow an hour each). Then we'll all get together for lunch in the executive dining room and cover whatever final questions she has and/or make our final points. Edna is familiar with the company. She wrote the initial story for the *Constitution,* when we launched three years ago and has done several follow-up pieces since then. Her reportage has been fair and accurate. Edna is a University of Georgia economics graduate, grew up in Danielsville, and joined the *Constitution* five years ago upon graduating from college. She is a solid and responsible reporter. These interviews are for a story planned for a Sunday edition of the *Constitution,* intended to play the week we release third quarter earnings. This will be a major profile on us, and consequently, of more than passing importance. Everything will be for-the-record, unless you specifically, and clearly, set it off-the-record or designate it for-non-attribution. Our practice, always, is to be on-the-record, unless there is an over-riding reason for using one of the other approaches.

This is our plan for approaching the story:

Jim will cover:
- Our basic philosophies and practices, particularly the "vision"—that is, what the company hopes to accomplish . . . its mission . . . its goals.
- He'll also handle the discussion of the Kildare Island Program . . . what it is, why it exists, its present status, and its near term plans. He'll focus particularly on the amount and types of investments being made in the Kildare Island area (housing, elderly independence, etc.)
- He'll explain what "results oriented" management means and how this concept defines the company's character and approach.
- He'll give his evaluation of how well this is progressing against plan to date.
- He'll handle the "management behavior" question as we've discussed.
- And then, of course, whatever questions are put to him.

Ed will cover:
- How the company is organized to do its jobs, including the criteria used in the selection of staff, the quality and credentials of the staff, the "non-traditional office" approach and why it's important, staff commitment and morale, and discuss how the organization has changed since start-up and what is expected to change in the near future.
- The company's values and how they drive operations.

- He'll also address, in his capacity as Chief Administrative Officer and Member of the Management Committee, the competence and effectiveness of the management of the Foundation to date in growing it from a start-up to an important and positive factor in its areas of focus.
- And whatever other questions are put to him.

Don will cover:

- The compelling story of the investments made to date, detailing the specific investments and highlighting their substance. He'll discuss how the project groups work individually and how they collaborate and discuss how communications flow to keep those who should be informed up-to-date and in the loop.
- How the company handles investigations and evaluates projects.
- He'll also detail the company's emphasis on its audit practices, reporting, and management oversight.
- And whatever questions are put to him.

Following are the general discussion areas the reporter has in mind and suggestions on key points to be made.

1. **How do you rate the company's performance so far?**

   The company is just a little over two years old. We are about at the end of our "start-up" phase—assembling a staff, getting settled in office spaces, setting objectives, establishing procedures, getting operating issues worked out, learning the territory—everything that's necessary to turn an idea into a functioning organization. We're about through that now. That's a relatively short time frame . . . like mid-way through the first inning. It's a little early to make judgments on how the game is likely to turn out. But so far, we're satisfied with our results.

2. **Are things going faster or slower than you expected when the company was organized?**

   On balance we are about where we should be at this stage of the game.
   The organizational set-up is sound.
   We've established solid criteria for finding and funding the projects that fit our objectives.
   We have an excellent and motivated staff.
   We've put important sums of money to work on important projects in our areas of focus.
   Our oversight procedures and audits are rigorous, both in terms of management review and reporting internally and in terms of the various reports and filings required by our charter (these are matters of public record and easily accessible.)
   Our management committee—Jim Sonsen (President), Ed Barton (Chief Administrative Officer), Don Penny (Chief Operating Officer) and Mary Jameson (Chief Financial Officer)—meets twice monthly. Regular monthly all-hands meetings with the full executive staff give everyone two-way updates on projects, problems and opportunities.

3. **Are the company's pay packages and executive perks in line with others in the industry?**

   Salaries at all levels are consistent with salary levels in the peer group. Annual bonuses based on performance are used as incentives with all staff—both exempt and non-exempt.

There is a modest stock option plan covering executives at the senior vice president level and above. We hope to extend this to all employees in time.

There are no perks . . . no automobiles, club memberships, etc., and everyone flies economy, except for international travel, where business-class seating is okayed.

4. **There has been criticism that you've let cronyism dominate your staffing actions, rather than going after the best talent available.**

In assembling a staff for a start-up, where getting up to speed as rapidly as possible is important, the best (and proven) practice is to bring in people whose track record and capabilities you're familiar with from personal experience because you've worked with them. You augment that group with highly competent people, recruited because they have the kind of record and credentials that say, on paper, they should be able to do the job.

That's what we've done. Our staff is a mixture of both. Some of the senior positions are held by people whom our CEO worked with or knew through professional association. Others have been recruited.

You need the mix because you don't have much time to experiment and you don't always know how people are going to work out.

5. **What's next, that is, what are your plans for the future?**

We're going to continue to go slowly. We want to make sure we understand each business line thoroughly before adding another and to have fully explored the business opportunities in each geographic area before expanding to others. Consequently, we don't see ourselves moving into any substantial new product areas for a year or so, and no geographic expansion for at least that long. That doesn't mean we won't grow. We'll increase our market share in each product line and geographic area aggressively. We want solid, steady growth, not mercurial ups and downs. We feel very good about our prospects.

# # #

INTERACTIVE EXERCISES CHAPTER 15

Briefing Papers and Q&As

Exercise One

You're preparing George Owsley, the president of the Iowa Seed Company (see chapter 14), for an interview with a *Houston Chronicle* business reporter on ISC's plan to expand into Texas and Oklahoma. Using the facts presented as background, write the Q&A you would propose, were you preparing Mr. Owsley for this interview. This will be the first interview with a major paper in one of the key areas of expansion, so it is important the interview goes well.

Exercise Two

Write a briefing paper for Mr. Owsley on the upcoming Dallas news conference, covering the points outlined in this chapter. Since all the details required for such a briefing paper aren't included in the chapter, you will need to use your imagination and to create them.

Use the CD-ROM to compare answers.

## CHAPTER SIXTEEN

PITCHES AND PRÉCIS: SELLING STORY IDEAS

People who make their living by writing are masters at selling story ideas. Those who do not work steadily for an organization of some type, such as a newspaper or magazine, a television station, or a not-for-profit, are called freelancers. Freelancers can't afford to invest time or effort in writing a piece in hopes it will sell. They must be assured of a sale before they write, especially since most unsolicited manuscripts are ignored or thrown out. On the other side of the equation, editors (the buyers) don't want to be bothered with material they haven't requested.

The solution for both the writer and the editor is the query letter.

Letter: "I have this idea for a story. Are you interested?"

Reply: "Sounds interesting. Give me 2,000 words." Or, "Thanks, but don't bother."

This is a very efficient practice. It works well for both parties.

Public relations writers working to place a significant article with a newspaper or magazine use a similar approach. Only in the case of public relations, you are not suggesting to the editor that you write the story (though you would and could, if asked). Instead, you are trying to interest the publication, or the writers with whom you're working, to do the story themselves. You're selling the story idea, not the finished product.

You do this through a "pitch letter" or a "précis." Pitch letters and précis (pronounced, pray-see) are essentially the same. Both are used to present story ideas for major articles in a way that garners attention. The most important single fact to remember about pitch letters or précis is that you must capture the editor's interest with the first line. Editors deal with hundreds of queries and pitches, so they can't waste time waiting for the story idea to become apparent. Make it apparent. Capture their attention.

WRITING PITCHES AND PRÉCIS

Effective pitch letters and précis are written as follows:

- Start with a lead paragraph that is phrased exactly as if it were the lead for the story you have in mind. It must be interesting, arresting, compelling copy, designed to draw the reader (and the editor) into the story.
- Next use a series of paragraphs to flesh out the story, detailing how it might unfold and highlighting the information that will appeal to the publication's readers.

- Follow with a short paragraph describing the experts available for interview and comment, the background information you've assembled to make the reporting easier, and the art or graphics that are available or can be developed to support and illustrate the piece. Also offer whatever cooperation is needed for the publication's writer to fully develop the story.
- Close with a paragraph that summarizes why the story is interesting or important to the readership, confirms that the story is an exclusive, and closes by asking for the order.

In essence, you're convincing the editor that you have an excellent story that will appeal to her readers, while assuring her it can be easily reported and written on an exclusive basis. This should be communicated in two pages of copy or less.

Sometimes you'll address your story précis to the editor, in hopes that he or she will see enough merit in it to assign a reporter. Sometimes you will take it directly to the reporter who covers your "beat." The format is slightly altered for the particular needs of broadcast, such as highlighting visuals in the case of television and sounds in the case of radio.

Know Your Target

Writing a successful précis requires you that you know what makes a story. Equally important, it requires that you also know what makes a story for the particular outlet you've targeted. You know this, because you've done the research necessary to understand the publication's readers. You know the types of stories it usually runs and the kinds of topics it covers. You've identified the editor or writer most likely to be receptive to your story idea through your assessment of previously published stories. And you are a good enough writer to cast your précis in the style most consistent with that of the publication.

A successful pitch letter also requires you to understand the competition the reporter or writer you want to work with is up against.

A writer or reporter makes his or her reputation by producing strong stories that appear in prominent locations in the publication or make it on-air. The writer or reporter is in constant competition for space and recognition. Your story idea has to be good enough to win out over all the other story ideas being promoted by other editors and writers that day or week. Do this and you will be a hero to both the writer and your client or organization.

The pitch letter that follows lays out a story idea for a local paper. The story, although presented with a local angle, has national ramifications. If the reporter is smart and ambitious, she will see the possibility for a free-lance piece for a national general readership publication and/or special publications in the psychology and education fields.

August 18, 2005

Shelly Andersen
The Boulder Daily Journal
178 Basalt Street
Boulder, CO 80210

Dear Shelly,

Ginny Simms tells it exactly like it is. She never pulls any punches, never dances around, and she isn't popular with the other kids. But, she can't help herself.

A bright, attractive 14-year-old at Orion School, Ginny is a victim of Asperger's Syndrome, until recently a misdiagnosed affliction affecting a surprising number of people young and old, and resulting in thwarted careers and blocked opportunities. The "Asperger's Kids" as they are called, are usually high IQ students with superior math and science skills who frustrate both teachers and parents by their lack of social and language skills and their single focus fixation on sometimes esoteric topics. Previously, they were being written off as "difficult" in the best of cases, and semi-autistic or with severe attention deficit disorder problems in the more severe. Recent advances in the understanding and treatment of the syndrome, though, are changing that and allowing their potential to be developed to their benefit and to that of society.

A new school here in Boulder is pioneering the way.

Shelley, we think what's happening with the recognition of Asperger's and the development of effective treatments can be an interesting and important story, not only for your readers, but possibly on the national level. Parents, educators, anyone who has come into contact with a very bright kid who can't seem to stay focused or be conversant with simple standards of manners, will all find an interest here.

Dr. Katherine Stewart, founder of Orion Schools, is the nation's ranking expert on the syndrome and is pioneering a new way of education for these potentially high contributing youngsters. She and her staff, as well as the research material they've developed, will be fully available to you, as will various students and parents involved with the school.

This is an important story. We've come to you first because we know your interest in education and family matters. If you would like to pursue the story, please let me know as soon as possible and we'll make the necessary arrangements.

Thanks for your time and consideration.

Sincerely,

Bill Edwards
Manager
(303) 788-2476 /email: be@clarkecom.net

INTERACTIVE EXERCISES CHAPTER 16

Pitches and Précis: Selling Story Ideas

Exercise One

A local women's specialty shop wants to launch a new line of costume jewelry handmade by a Navajo teenager of the Taos Pueblo. The jewelry—bracelets and necklaces—features a design believed to be of Anasazi origin. Originally discovered by the teenager on the wall of a hidden cave on a deserted mesa on the reservation, these designs have never been seen before. The design shows a crescent moon cradled in the widespread wings of an eagle. The teenager, a girl named Rebecca, is the third of five children (three girls and two boys). She is 16 years old and is graduating from high school this year. If the jewelry is successful, the income will pay her way through college and be used to establish college funds for her siblings. Your public relations firm has been hired to gain national recognition for the jewelry, creating interest that can lead to sales.

A. Which print media do you target for this story? (Types of print media, not specific outlets, i.e., fashion editors of daily newspapers.)

B. Does the story have several levels that will allow it to be pitched to more than one print outlet without impinging on exclusivity?

C. Are there TV possibilities here?

Exercise Two

Write:

A. The opening paragraphs of a précis for *seventeen* magazine, based on the jewelry story.

B. The opening paragraphs of a précis for *The Albuquerque Journal Sunday Magazine*.

Use the CD-ROM to check your answers.

## CHAPTER SEVENTEEN

WRITING FOR THE INTERNET

When you write for the Internet, you are doing so for people who actively seek information. This means you are writing for hunters, or those who want their information fast, straight and accurate. They also want it in a format that's easy to access and assimilate.

This presents a particularly interesting challenge for professionals who do the kind of writing featured in this book. The ability to assemble and package facts in a persuasive manner without benefit of rhetoric is no small feat. Though rhetoric is an honorable tool, one that the best players in the field master and use adroitly, we must put it aside when we write for the Internet.

The ability to write high-quality content specifically for the Internet is, or soon will be, one of those specialized skills on a par with speechwriting and writing for the financial community.

FOCUS ON RELEVANCE, BREVITY AND PUNCH

The principles of producing good copy for the Internet are essentially the same as for all forms previously mentioned. The basic difference is the need for an unwavering focus on content relevance, brevity and punch.

The Internet landscape is littered with so much information that unless you capture your visitor's attention almost immediately, you are probably going to lose the overall battle for his or her attention. You must find a way to provide your information in easily digestible bites, or he or she is going to find information elsewhere.

Since most Internet users scan rather than read, your information and arguments must be presented in a way that capitalizes on this fact. Research shows that reading on screen can be as much as 25 percent slower than reading a printed page, but that the Internet reader is no more patient than a print reader in wanting the information. As a result, your Internet copy must be even more concise than that for print and, given the impatience factor, marginally more appealing. Be clear here that we are talking about content preparation and not Web page design. Content preparation works in tandem with, but should not be confused with, the technical work of constructing and managing Web sites.

To follow are some basic principles for handling the public relations writing aspects involved in preparing content for the Web.

THE GUIDELINES

How can you best prepare your information for the Internet?

- Make the headline compelling. It is all-important. If you don't grab your reader with the header, you have probably missed your chance.
- Keep the text short and to the point. Remember, many other tempting distractions are just a mouse click away.
- Use short, simple, understandable words, and fashion short, simple, understandable sentences.
- Make your points quickly and succinctly.
- Let no story run longer than a single page; shorter is always better.
- Limit each paragraph in a story to a single idea.
- Use conversational phrasing.
- Build your story on the inverted pyramid framework, beginning with the most important point on top, with remaining material presented in descending order of importance (the classic news writing style), so readers can follow as far as your material, or their interest, takes them.
- Present your information in digestible bites that can be easily scanned. Elements that promote this are:
    1. provocative headlines,
    2. concise and informative subheads,
    3. highlighted text,
    4. bulleted lists, and
    5. topic sentences displayed in boldface.
- Try to provide the "right" amount of information. In other words, provide enough information for your readers to understand and be adequately informed on the topic, but not so much information as to cause their eyes to glaze over. Your job is to help make a reader reasonably well-informed, but not necessarily an expert. If more than one page of copy is required, stay with the one-idea-per-paragraph rule and keep presenting information in descending order of importance.

In addition:

- Do not allow anything that remotely resembles advertising or "selling" to invade your copy.
- Take maximum advantage of good graphics and visuals to support your story and to capture interest.
- Include links to other sites that lead readers to additional sources of information and expand and enrich the story (this is a powerful tool that allows you to get persuasive arguments and additional supporting information in front of your reader without treading on the "Just the facts" edict).
- Check and double-check all facts. Errors are not permissible.
- And most important, remember what you're trying to achieve. You're not doing this for amusement. You're trying to make something happen.

Take the Johnson & Johnson Web page below as a first rate example of Internet writing. The information is concise yet thorough, and the page displays current news along with portals to detailed information about the company.

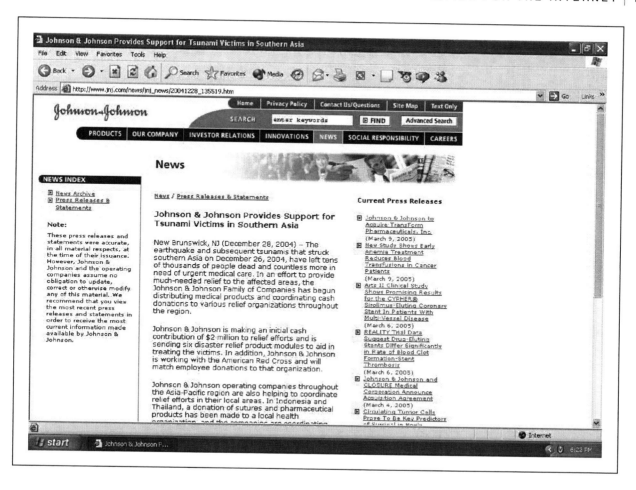

INTERACTIVE EXERCISES CHAPTER 17

Writing for the Internet

Exercise One

Assume you are writing for the ISC Web site. Write an "about us" paragraph as the lead item for the opening page of the Web site using the guidelines in this chapter.

Exercise Two

Go online and pull up the Web pages of General Motors, The Port of Stockton, *The St. Louis Post-Dispatch*, Kaiser-Permanente, the American Youth Soccer Association (AYSA), and the Kentucky Department of Fish and Wildlife Resources. Note the content and design of each and do a brief paper explaining, in your opinion, the target audience each seeks. Be sure to include the reasons why you've come to these conclusions.

Use the CD-ROM to check your responses.

## CHAPTER EIGHTEEN

WRITING FOR CRISIS MANAGEMENT AND DAMAGE CONTROL SITUATIONS

Because so much fundamental change is occurring so rapidly in the opening years of the 21st century, crises have become a matter of "business as usual" for many organizations. Consequently, crisis management and damage control have become an integral part of the portfolio of public relations professionals. They are expected to be prepared to effectively handle crises when they occur. Note that the term is "when," not "if." Be relatively confident that at some point in your career, you will be called upon to handle a crisis.

Aggressive communications during a crisis is crucially important, and writing is the key tool in making the communications effort successful.

There is no intention in this short chapter to cover the theory and practice of crisis management and damage control. Entire books and semester-long college courses are devoted to the subject. Rather, this information is simply an introduction to the type of writing required for the successful management of crisis situations.

Ideally, this brand of writing is an end product of a thoughtful and established crisis management plan. For the most part, crisis communications will be executed by seasoned professionals, who have the full confidence of management. Depending on circumstances, however, junior members of the public relations staff may find themselves pressed into duty, and in smaller organizations with limited staff, the responsibility can fall to whomever is there, until experienced help can be brought in to assist.

CRISES COME IN TWO VARIETIES

You must have at least a rudimentary understanding of the "what" and "how" of crisis management and damage control, lest you be put on the firing line totally unprepared.

Crises come in two varieties. One is the "surprise" variety. No one sees it coming. No one expects it. Crises of this type are usually the result of natural disasters (e.g., floods, earthquakes, hurricanes) or accidents (e.g., chemical spills, equipment malfunctions, explosions).

The second crisis is of the "we-ought-to-have-been-smart-enough-to-see-this-coming-but-didn't" variety. These are almost always the result of bad decisions, bad planning, bad execution, and either stupidity or greed, or both. In this category are examples like the Enron implosion, the Exxon Valdez oil spill, the Vioxx recall, and most of the others you see in the news with increasing regularity.

Another important thing to understand is that while all crises share certain similarities, each one is different. Consequently, they cannot be handled with a pre-designed formula.

THE FUNDAMENTALS OF CRISIS MANAGEMENT

There are, however, certain fundamentals that work in almost all cases:

1. Take control of the information flow. Establish one point-of-contact within your organization where all information can be collected, verified and held, and from which all comment is issued. Use only one source, or spokesperson, for the media. Make sure all media inquiries are directed to that individual.

2. Keep employees informed. Brief them frequently, so everyone is "speaking with one voice," and so they may respond with accuracy when asked questions.

3. Take the initiative. Release your side of the story as quickly as possible. If you tell it first, you get to define the problem. Equally as important, you want to be on the offensive, not the defensive. Leading the way with volunteered information is a materially stronger position than appearing as if you're hiding and waiting for questions.

4. Tell what you know, when you know it. Don't feel the need to wait until you have every detail. Things move too quickly. If you pass up an opportunity to make your points, because you don't yet have all the information, you may miss it forever. Release the facts as you know them, when you know them. If subsequent developments prove them to be inaccurate, correct them at that time. In fluid situations, a little information is better than none.

5. Share your bad news as soon as possible. Get it over with and behind you. Trying to sit on bad news invites disaster. The rule is, "Get your own bad news on and off the front page as fast as possible." Better yet, avoid the front page!

6. Tell it like it is. Don't dance, dissemble or try to be clever.

7. Tell people what's being done to fix the problem. Tell it as rapidly and as widely as you can. And don't assume that once it has been said, everyone knows. Keep detailing the steps you're taking, until the crisis is over.

8. Take your story directly to your constituents. Don't rely on the media to do this for you. The media's job is to report a story, not necessarily "your" story. Getting your message across to the people whose opinions and actions can make a difference is too important to be left to others. Use the communication tools available to you and go to your stakeholders directly, in your own words, and repeatedly.

9. Try to do what's right, however bad the problem. If people believe you're really trying to do the right thing in fixing the issue, you will be given the benefit of the doubt. If they don't, you will receive no sympathy or leeway. The public can be very forgiving, unless it smells a cover-up.

10. BE READY. This probably should have led the list, but it's here at the end for emphasis. Always assume that at any given time, any of the landmines that have knowingly or unknowingly been planted by your people, your operations, the economy, or the environment might explode. Savvy organizations understand this and have established a general plan for crisis management and damage control. Such a plan is updated regularly, with communications channels set, a spokesperson designated, subject matter experts briefed and available, and procedures for controlling the information flow established. *Be ready!*

COMMUNICATIONS IN THE CRISIS MODE

From the writer's standpoint, the principal forms used in the crisis communication are:

- News releases,
- Statements,
- Q&As and FAQs,
- Background and briefing papers, and
- Letters.

Use releases to distribute breaking news as it develops. Written statements are used to update the media on the situation or in explanation of actions being taken. These are most particularly useful when you do not want to send a release or provide someone for an interview. The Q&As and FAQs are to be used for those being interviewed by the media, or they can be sent out to make contact with employees, community or customer groups. Background and briefing papers are used for key constituencies, as they define the issues and actions in terms you know to be accurate. Letters are useful in making specific points, in a personal way, directly to key contacts like shareholders, elected officials, community leaders and employees.

Releases should be tightly written and unambiguous. Statements offer some latitude for a bit of explanation and editorializing, while Q&As and FAQs offer the greatest flexibility. The background and briefing papers let you set the framework for what happened and why, and explain what you're doing to fix the problem. The letters provide a way to tell your version of the story at any and every stage of the exercise, taking advantage of a personal tone, and ideally, winning friends and influencing people.

In any crisis situation, you'll have to be fast and thorough. There's no room to be lame or tentative. You also will have to be confident enough in your own capabilities, as no one has time for handholding when a crisis is in progress. There will be confusion, pressure and considerable uncertainty. You must handle them all.

Few things can advance a career as rapidly as a well-handled crisis. No other single challenge in public relations requires the combination of mental and professional ability, creative and analytical reach, judgment, character, personality and stamina that crisis management requires. People who possess these qualities are in high demand.

For examples of how crisis communications pieces look and read, see the following. The first is an example of a combination standby statement and Q&A for a winery in the early stages of what might be a controversial lawsuit. The second is a fact sheet to be used if the controversy moves to trial. The issue is the safety and quality of Mountain Crest wines, which Carrington has criticized in public comment and for which, his suit claims, he was discharged.

Standby Statement and Q&A Talk Sheet
For use *verbally* in response to media queries

RE: THE CARRINGTON CASE

Assuming a query along the lines of "I understand an employee is going to bring suit for wrongful discharge for whistle-blowing re: the operations at the winery . . ."

Standby statement: "A lawyer representing a recently discharged employee sent us a letter threatening that unless we paid a large sum of money to his client, he would not only file a lawsuit against us but would put out information designed to trash the reputation of our wine. We found this tactic offensive and the allegations outrageous. We, of course, refused to pay anything. We have confidence in the excellence of our wine and are confident we have acted properly in all regards. We're equally confident that if a suit is filed, any court or jury will reach the same conclusions. This is, at present, a private matter and we are not releasing the name of the employee or his attorney."

Q1 If pressed—are you saying "blackmail"?
A1 "No, I'm merely telling you what seemed to be the substance of the letter."
Q2 If pressed for more details—i.e., "what's this all about?"
A2 "An employee was discharged for cause. I can't be more specific than that. These situations are private matters between employee and employer. If this becomes a public matter through a suit, then those details will, of course, be made public."
Q4 If pressed for specific details on other matters—acidity, bacterial count, safety, etc.
A4 "I'd have to see the particulars of a suit to comment, but if it comes to a legal action, our attorneys will do the talking. Let me just say in general that the winery, gladly, meets all state and federal requirements and any suggestion to the contrary is nonsense. The proof is in the quality of our wines, which both consumers and industry experts consistently rank as world class."

# # #

Media Fact Sheet re: Carrington Case

FACTS RELATING TO THE CARRINGTON SUIT

For further information:
John Constantine
Mountain Crest Winery
(707-831-2000)

1. Carrington was terminated for cause. The law prohibits any discussion on our part about the facts upon which the termination was based except in court. The pertinent information will be provided there.

2. VA (volatile acidity) is an important component of quality wines. VA levels vary from barrel to barrel in wines prior to blending. Some are high, some are low. These differences are married to produce the desired level during the process of making the finished wine. This is part of the art of winemaking. The important VA measure, therefore, is that of the finished wine. VA levels are regulated for quality, not health, reasons. Mountain Crest wines meet all applicable federal and state standards. As important, they meet the quality standards of the marketplace as evidenced by the continuing strong demand for our wine by consumers.

3. Mountain Crest wines are, in effect, "hand-made." They are produced in small batches and crafted to deliver a very special taste experience. Mountain Crest's red wines are made using an old Burgundian method that allows for more gentle fermentation. The process is called "punch cap." In the red wine-making process, a "cap" of skins and pulp form over the fermenting grapes. That cap needs to be broken from time to time to allow fermentation to continue successfully. In the punch cap method, grapes are fermented in small tanks and the cap is actually broken and the mixture stirred by hand. This is not a standard winemaking process today. It is labor intensive, requires close personal attention, is done in small batches and, therefore, doesn't offer the advantages of scale that deliver the sorts of economic returns the more profit-oriented wineries require. Bigger operations use a different process, ferment in tanks often 15 times larger than Mountain Crest's, and break the cap mechanically.

4. The barrels in which Mountain Crest wines are aged are hand-crafted from special woods. The barrels affect the quality of the wine, which fact Mountain Crest uses in shaping its wines. Mountain Crest matches certain woods, themselves aged over the years, with certain wines to achieve the desired taste result. The barrels and the aging process fully meet all state and federal standards—as do Mountain Crest's operations overall.

INTERACTIVE EXERCISES CHAPTER 18

Writing for Crisis Management and Damage Control Situations

Exercise One

A. The chapter lists the five principal writing forms most typically employed in crisis situations. What are they and how are they used?

B. The chapter outlines the fundamentals to be applied in any crisis situation. What are they?

Exercise Two

The "Golden Rule" of crisis management is: "Get control of the information flow, take the initiative, and tell the truth." Often this can mean releasing bad news before anyone knows about it. How do you feel about this? Write a short paragraph or two summarizing your thoughts.

Exercise Three

Assume a local reporter has confirmed that Carrington's attorney has shown him a copy of a lawsuit for wrongful discharge, which he will file in county court tomorrow. Assume, as well, that you want to minimize the coverage that would flow from the filing of a lawsuit. You decide to take the initiative and issue a pre-emptive release this afternoon that will put the winery on record first and provide it the chance to position the story. Using the information and tone contained in the standby statement and talk sheet, write the first two paragraphs of that release.

Use the CD-ROM to check your responses.

## CHAPTER NINETEEN

WRITING SPEECHES

Of all the special writing skills public relations writers must acquire, speech writing may be the most difficult. But it has its rewards. Really good speechwriters are among the best paid in the business.

Those who practice speechwriting as a full-time pursuit have first-rate minds, are inordinately well-read and well-informed, delight in using language effectively and persuasively, and have an academic's commitment to ideas and a researcher's tenacity for fact. They delight in fashioning arguments that win or convince.

Not many people become full-time speechwriters. There aren't that many full-time jobs available and not enough good people available to make a career of it.

However, almost all public relations writers, at one time or another, will be called upon to write a speech, for the boss, for executives representing the organization before this group or that, or even for themselves. In organizations without full-time speech writers, the chore falls within the public relations function.

THE MECHANICS ARE SIMPLE

The mechanics of speech writing are fairly simple; execution presents the challenge.

In a speech, any speech, you have information to impart or an idea to sell. As with other forms of public relations writing, you are trying to make something happen. Your best chance to do this is to marshal your ideas in a logical chain, package them in words that make your points clearly and persuasively, present it well and ask for the order.

Let's say you've been assigned to write a speech for Iowa Seed Company's marketing manager, who has accepted an invitation to address the Future Farmers of America in Austin, Texas. Before you begin writing, you need to research the organization and form an idea of how its members can be helpful to ISC's plans in Texas.

Once you know this, you can structure the speech to maximize the company's investment of time and effort.

KNOW THE AUDIENCE

Before you begin writing, you'll need a firm grasp on the goals of ISC for its expansion into Texas. This must be balanced with an understanding of what the group to whom you're speaking wants to hear about. The easiest way to do so is to speak with the individual who issued the invitation to see if he or she had something specific in mind. While doing this, make sure to glean as much detailed information about the group as possible. In this case, helpful information would include the number of members, what schools they attend, the kind of projects they are involved in, the age range of the members, and details on previous speakers and their topics. Most often, invitations to speak are issued on a "talk about anything you like" basis. And that's fine, because those types of invitations allow you to maximize your company's goals and agenda. Remember, if you are going to invest the company's time and money, you want to insure a return. Toward that end, you would be sure to consult various subject-matter experts in ISC to get their ideas on what topics and information should be highlighted and emphasized. In addition, you should conduct your own research on issues or concerns current to the Austin area, that could have implications to your speech. When you have gathered all relevant information, you're ready to start structuring the speech.

THE "TELL THEM" RULE AND THE "RULE OF THREE"

An old, but very good rule about writing speeches is to "tell them what you're going to tell them, tell them, and then tell them what you've told them." In doing so, you must not go overboard and try to tell them too much. The "rule of three" always applies. Using more than three key points to support your basic message is counterproductive. You need strong points, but not so many that the listener has to struggle to retain them. Hit your points clean and hard, but limit them to those that are most important. This means, of course, that you must be rigorous in the development of your argument.

Another rule to treasure is KISS, the old "keep it short and keep it simple" principle. Complex ideas do not resonate well with audiences who don't have the appropriate background or little or no interest in the subject. Research shows what we all know to be true: most people have short attention spans. Speeches that run much longer than 25 minutes won't hold an audience. They simply stop listening as their minds begin to wander. You can avoid the perils of inattention through the engaging and articulate delivery of an unusually compelling idea. Even so, keeping it short and simple are good practices.

Begin writing the speech by outlining the ideas you intend to present and the order in which they'll be presented. An outline helps insure arguments lead logically and understandably from one point to the next, and build to a conclusion that will be both logical and persuasive. The outline also insures that you have a firm grasp on the ideas you want to market.

As in all the other writing we've talked about, your first job is to capture and hold the audience's attention. To do so, you need a "hook," a good strong opening statement. But be careful that you don't set it right away. Audiences must settle a little before they are ready to begin paying attention, so have the speaker spend a few moments talking about how glad he is to be there, thanking the club for the invitation, commenting on the weather, or making reference to something of current local interest. Such statements allow the audience to realize that someone is standing before them and talking. Only when you have their attention should you begin the real speech.

A TEMPLATE FOR A SPEECH

Winston Churchill, one of the greatest speakers of all time, said, "If you have an important point to make, don't try to be subtle or clever. Use a pile driver. Hit the point once. Then come back and hit it again. Then hit it a third time—a tremendous whack!"

With repetition in mind, follow the following guidelines when constructing your speech:

- Begin with a few let-them-get-settled and get-their-attention remarks
- Set the hook
- Tell them what you're going to tell them
- Tell them
- Summarize by telling them what you've told them
- Ask for the order in closing

Never make the mistake of regarding this formula as being too simplistic. Repetition is a building block of learning, a key tactic in advertising that sells.

In all cases except those involving matters of high consequence, keep the tone of the speech conversational and, to the extent possible, personalize the content. To do so, use short declarative sentences. Stay away from circumlocutions or pretentious phrases, and inject a little humor where appropriate. Humor makes the speaker more likeable, and likeable people are always more believable.

The best way to test whether or not the tone is conversational is to read the copy aloud. If it sounds strained, stilted or unclear, it is.

Once the speech is written, circulate it to the subject-matter experts with whom you consulted and ask if they feel the points are correct and well made. If they don't, keep working with them and with the copy until they are comfortable.

Speeches are developed in either one of two ways: 1) full text, that is, a fully scripted speech that the speaker will read from, or 2) a talking outline, which lists the points to be made and the order in which the points are to be presented. This format allows the speaker to "just talk," but even so, the key points are fully scripted. No one ad-libs the most memorable phrases. To get it right, it has to be written.

Reading copies (the copy of the text from which the speaker will read) of fully scripted speeches are prepared on standard letter size paper. The text is double-spaced in 16-point type or larger. The larger type makes it easier for the speaker to read and keep his place as he maintains eye contact with the audience. Talking outline texts are sometimes put on five-by-seven inch cards in 14-point type. This permits the speaker to hold the cards in one hand while she moves about and frees her from being "locked" to a lectern.

SCRIPTING SOMETHING THAT SOMEONE ELSE CAN DELIVER

One of the biggest challenges in speech writing is producing a script that someone else can deliver effectively. Most people are a bit intimidated by having to stand up and speak in public, especially if they must read from a prepared text. They become nervous and tentative. They read with little or no intonation. Their pronunciation is uncertain, their voice flat and manner weak.

To help the speaker overcome these impediments, beginning speech writers are often advised to try to write as the person for whom they are writing talks, the idea being to make it natural and easy. Unfortunately, just as most people are less than compelling speakers, most are not spellbinding conversationalists either. The better advice, therefore, is to write the speech not as the speaker would ordinarily converse, but to write it *in phrases that make the points as effectively as possible in language and phrasing the speaker can handle comfortably.* The speaker has a lot at stake when standing before an audience, and he or she wants to come across as knowledgeable, authoritative, likeable and articulate. Help the speaker achieve this. Don't write it the way he or she would say it. Instead, write it the way *it should be said* in words he or she can deliver convincingly.

The success of a speech is measured by the way it is received, which largely depends on how the message is packaged and delivered. Churchill said, "There are three keys to a good speech. The first is what is said. The second is who said it. The third is how it is said. Of the three, the latter is the most important." The way ideas are expressed, the words and images used, and the way the speaker delivers them can make speeches most memorable. Well said, well remembered.

THE IMPORTANCE OF REHEARSAL

You don't have much control over delivery. You can better control delivery through practice, or rehearsal. Never, if you can avoid it, send anyone to deliver an unrehearsed speech. The rehearsal need not be anything complicated. Assemble one or two people in a small room somewhere and have the speaker deliver the full text exactly as he or she would deliver it on the actual occasion. If the phrasing or the order of presentation doesn't seem to be effective, rework them. Rehearse again. Lock it down. The hour or two invested in this exercise is invaluable.

A tightly focused speech program designed to deliver important messages through well prepared speakers to audiences whose opinions and actions make a difference, can be one of the most effective, and least costly, public relations initiatives.

SHAPERS AND ARTICULATORS

Organizations that understand and use the speech-making tool effectively typically have on staff one or two good writers with strong ideas and personalities. These professionals understand their organization thoroughly. They see the world realistically. They have wide-ranging intellectual interests. Because they are knowledgeable and bright and have good ideas, they are able to establish close working relationships with the people for whom they write. As a result, they operate in the most senior and confidential spheres of the organization. At this level, they become shapers and articulators of the organization's most important ideas and principles.

All speeches are important, no matter how brief the comments or small the audience. So give all speeches careful attention and apply the effort needed to achieve the result you seek.

A caution as this section ends: do not try to write a speech without having studied the construction of good examples. You may be a natural, but even so, a little exploration never hurts. Read a few first-rate speeches. A service called *Vital Speeches of the Day* regularly collects and reprints from around the nation what it considers the best and most significant non-political speeches given each month. Your library, or an online search, can find it for you. Or check out a copy of *The World's Great Speeches*, edited by Copeland and Lamm and published by Dover.

In the meantime, the following is an example of a formal speech aimed at a special group of teenagers, but with important implications for much wider audiences.

THE POWER AND THE GLORY
Finding the Intersection of Individualism and Interdependence in Our Global.com Village

Remarks

BY
TEVEIA R. BARNES, ESQ.
EXECUTIVE DIRECTOR
LAWYERS FOR ONE AMERICA

BEFORE THE

24TH ANNUAL
United Nations International School-
- United Nations
CONFERENCE
NEW YORK, NY

Thank you, Anna, for that very generous introduction. I hardly recognize myself!

Honorable members of the General Assembly; members of the diplomatic corps; distinguished guests, including those watching and listening on the Internet and UN media around the globe; and the hundreds of students in this historic hall:

It is an honor and a pleasure to be with you today. Speaking at the United Nations is a dream-come-true for me. I am particularly pleased to be part of this UNIS-UN conference on Global Interdependence and Inequalities, and amazed to be able to talk to 700 teenagers simultaneously. Given that at home I often cannot get the full attention of my two teenage sons, this is truly awesome!

My sons Aaron and Zachary, my husband Alan, and our New York family . . . Ken, Susan, Genna, Lindsey, Alyssa, Lisa, and Don are here with me today. I wish to thank them for being with me and lending their support.

I want to talk to you about finding the intersection of your individual dreams and interdependence in our global.com village. Kind of like earlier generations found Broadway and 42nd St. in New York, or Abbey Road and Grove End in London, or Hollywood and Vine in L.A.

I'm going to spend a few minutes telling you about the intersections in my own life and what I learned from them, because it sets the stage for my main theme. Understanding the world you're inheriting—the good, the bad, and the ugly, and the power and the glory of finding your place, with knowledge of yourself.

In spite of all those accomplishments Anna mentioned in my introduction, I am really a one-note song. All my life, I only wanted to be one thing. And that is a lawyer. Not because of the prestige or pay check. Something else fueled my desire.

From the time I can remember, I dreamed of being an advocate for people who could not advocate for themselves. By the time I got to be your age, I was the one the other kids came to in school to settle disputes. They didn't always like my answers. Once someone who did not like my answer beat me up. Fortunately, I was rescued by the rest of my classmates, who thought a live mediator was better than a dead know-it-all.

At that intersection of my life, I learned the value of friendship and trust. More important, I learned that in a dispute, everyone has to walk away with something positive, with some level of dignity.

In retrospect, faith was the first intersection in my life journey. It gave me a moral basis to decide right from wrong, to live and let live, to practice ethical decision-making—the importance of always trying to do the right thing.

I also learned that I was a small piece of a great universe, but that I was a *vital* piece, and that my actions mattered.

Later, when I went to college, I gravitated toward activities that aimed at helping other people—from working at the women's clinic to tutoring other students who needed additional assistance. But when I graduated, with my dream set on going to law school, I could not get a summer job to make the money I needed. No where. No how. No one would hire me even though I had done very well at Rice University, a prestigious school. I had graduated with a triple major in Economics, German Studies and Political Science. I even had outstanding recommendations from professors.

From that intersection, I learned that what I perceived to be discrimination in not being hired was something more basic: the fact that no one wanted to hire a short-term bright kid on her way to law school, demanding college-level wages, no less. I learned that sometimes what looks like discrimination is actually just being the wrong person for the job, or not having the right credentials. Sometimes life is all about having Plan B—at least for awhile. So that summer, I formed my own company, "Teveia's Haberdashery", and made and sold hats, halters and purses. I had a good time and made a few dollars. So plan B actually turned out to be the best plan for me that summer. Sometimes the detour can be the real journey.

At the end of that summer, I did go to New York University Law School, and I did become a lawyer. I eventually settled in the legal department of BankAmerica, one of the largest banks in the world, where I came to head Global Corporate Banking and the International Division of the Legal Department.

International law forced me to deal with ethical conundrums, such as:

- Is it acceptable to offer bribes to get business done where that is the long-accepted custom?
- Is it acceptable to take deposits that are likely based on the profits of questionable activities?
- Is it acceptable to violate individuals' privacy to track potentially illegal activities?
- And is it acceptable to focus on only serving the rich, at the risk of discriminating against the rest?

At that intersection of my life, I learned always to strive for the moral, ethical and legally correct position. I learned that human principles transcend borders, and that it is important to fully appreciate and respect people's differences in this complex world. I truly believe that my values and my choices to do the right thing account for much of my success.

I now head a group called Lawyers for One America, a unique collaboration of legal professionals trying to change the landscape for racial justice in America. Our segregated schools, our redlined inner cities, our harassed and exploited immigrant communities tell us that we are not One America yet. Not when only 2% of the partners in America's largest law firms are people of color, even though profits are soaring in the legal industry.

The legal profession has been challenged by President Clinton to do good by doing what is right. That means increasing free legal services to people and communities of color and increasing diversity within the legal profession. I am proud to report that we are vigorously answering the President's call to help overcome this country's growing racial disparities, much as lawyers had done during the civil rights movement.

Hopefully, some of you sitting in this great hall will choose the hard but meaningful work of fighting for those who otherwise would have no access to our system of justice.

I now feel that I've come full circle, but with a wonderfully different perspective and a full measure of real-world experience gained in the 20+ years since law school.

I also learned, as I was working on this speech, that my childhood dream has come true. I realized that I have become what I envisioned and longed to be, a lawyer who advocates for her clients, with all their different needs and multiple perspectives.

That's been my journey, so far.

Now, what about you? What will be the crucial intersections in your life? How will you realize your dreams? What is the world going to be like for you? How can you, as one person, begin to redress the world's inequalities?

Let me suggest that a starting point for you might be the intersection of demographics and wealth in our global.com village:

There are 6 billion people in the world—double what we were one generation ago. Of every ten people, 6 are yellow, 2-1/2 are white, and 1-1/2 are brown. By 2050, we'll be 9 billion strong, with almost all the growth coming from what used to be called Lesser Developed Countries, — and now are known as "pre-consumer economies" by some global marketing firms.

Now in 2000, 20% of the world population that lives in high-income countries enjoys 80% of the world Gross Domestic Product, 82% of world exports, and 88% of the Internet connections. By 2001, the gap between rich and poor will become a chasm.

All too often, the color line determines who is rich and who is poor; who lives in luxury and who lives on the street; who will get food, clothing and health care; and all too often, who will live and who will die.

And as a woman of color, need I remind anyone hearing my voice that the burden of inequality is placed mostly on the backs of women of color? That women of color, by the tens of millions, hold the worst jobs and are the most exploited group in society? Even in America, in the most prosperous economy ever, unequal pay will cost the average 25-year-old working woman more than a half million dollars over her worklife.

There are many ways these facts, in turn, are going to intersect the future. Former US Labor Secretary Robert Reich has suggested one I particularly like. Secretary Reich thinks that those demographic and economic forces will play out against an increasing tension between *technology* and *tribalism* as the century unfolds.

Technology—especially two-way digital voice and imaging—is linking us all in real time to everything and everyone we could possibly want to be linked with. Technology is empirical—it's based on knowledge, rationality, and reasoned insight.

Tribalism is a very different force. It is based on human commonality—on language, religion, ethnicity, and homeland. Tribalism comes from the heart—from passion, from living, and from myth.

Neither technology nor tribalism is purely good or purely bad. As Reich says, the central dilemma of the 21st century will be finding the intersection between how to gain the material advantages of technology, while maintaining the human bonds and stable communities that give life enduring meaning.

You are living through a great technology revolution. A pocket calculator now has more power than John Glenn had in his Mercury space capsule orbiting the earth. The mapping of the human genome is virtually complete, and the possibility of human cloning is almost a reality.

Yet that same technological genius also has produced smart bombs and ever-escalating weapons of destruction. And it can do very little indeed to mediate the inevitable tribal conflicts yet to come.

Our greatest challenge in creating new forms of communications technology is ensuring that our humanity is not lost in the translation.

The tension between technology and tribalism will escalate as national borders become ever less relevant for money, goods, services and people; while at the same time, people yearn to define themselves and control their destinies. Technology also will push to homogenize global culture, yet paradoxically provide the means for people separated to remain connected to their cultures and to each other.

I was shocked to find out that "Baywatch" is the most widely viewed television program in the world! And that McDonald's opens a new outlet every 5 hours—about the time it takes to digest a hamburger! That seems almost obscene against the mortal facts that one in every six people worldwide suffers from acute or chronic hunger, and more than one billion are malnourished.

According to the United Nations 1998 Human Development Report, basic health and nutrition around the world would cost $13 billion dollars a year—about $4 billion dollars less than Americans and Europeans spend on *pet food*!

The UN Report also had this stunning statistic: basic education around the world would cost $6 billion a year—$2 billion dollars less than we spend in the United States on *cosmetics*.

That is much to consider. When you leave here today, many of your lives will intersect with other issues of your homelands or other places dear to you:

- Rwanda, where 80% of the young men have been killed in genocidal fury. Where young women have to choose between an almost certain diagnosis of AIDS spread by the few men left and having a child, a family, a future.
- China, where Internet access doubled in the last 6 months of 1999, to 9 million users, and the government struggles to control content.

- Afghanistan, where the Taliban has set up government and empowered Islamic religious police to enforce codes of dress and behavior that are especially restrictive to women.
- And here our beloved America, where senseless violence permeates every part of our society and the fate of a small Cuban boy mesmerizes, and polarizes, our citizens.

So how to think about all this? How do you build a framework to think, to argue, to intersect the issues of your times?

I cannot tell you how to live your lives—I can't tell my own sons that. But I can tell you that we need each of you. We need your energy and your insight. We very much need your sense of justice, and absolutely your vision of how things can be—how they *should* be. Most of all, we need your youthful idealism and belief in yourselves.

The only gift I can give you in return for asking me here today, and listening to me here today, is the gift of my experience. I have five things to offer you on your journeys:

Whatever you decide to do with your lives, figure out what your passion is, what you're good at because you love it, what makes you smile, and pursue it.

Cross-train your brain. Never stop learning, challenging, and doing. As the Dot.com Generation, find a need and fill it. Do not opt out.

Never underestimate the power of one. As Anne Frank wrote in her famous diary: "Isn't it nice to know that no one has to wait a single minute to start making the world a better place."

Strengthen yourself through your relationships. Develop a sense of who you are and what you are worth. And see and value others, as they truly are—not simply as a reflection of you.

And remember that you are truly citizens of interdependent global villages . . . if not *united* nations, then its tribes.

I will close my speech by talking about a remarkable human being—Mary McLeod Bethune. This great African American woman dedicated her life to bringing opportunity to other African-Americans. She integrated the Red Cross, and founded the National Council of Negro Women.

She advised US President Franklin D. Roosevelt, and, as many of you know, Mary Bethune also was a consultant on interracial affairs and understanding at the charter conference of the United Nations.

This is what she left in her last will and testament 45 years ago, and what I wish in turn to leave to each of the 700 students here today, to the honorable members of the General Assembly, and to those watching and listening on the Internet and UN communications channels throughout the world:

"I leave you love. I leave you hope. I leave you the challenge of developing confidence in one another. I leave you a thirst for education. I leave you a respect for the use of power. I leave you faith. I leave you racial dignity. I leave you a desire to live harmoniously with your fellow man. I leave you, finally, a responsibility to our young people."

As for me, I leave each of you with this one wish today, on the cusp of your life journey and at the intersection of the 21st century:

I wish for you to become everything that you are, but to leave no one behind. Thank you. I'd love to answer any questions you may have.

The previous example is a formal speech and reproduced in a format suitable for distribution to various audiences.

The next example is a talking outline for a speech. This format would be used if the speaker is to speak informally from notes instead of working from a formal text. Even so, note that many of the important points have been fully phrased. Though the example covers a presentation before a student group, the format works well in any circumstance where informality is desired or when carefully worded phrasing isn't required.

If the speaker will use a podium or lectern, or is going to speak while seated at a table (not recommended), the material can be formatted on standard-size paper. Otherwise, put the material on file cards, which are easier to handle, if standing or moving, and less noticeable.

TALKING NOTES:
EDWARDS UNIVERSITY
PUBLIC RELATIONS CLASS
JIM ATHERTON

TIPS FOR GETTING THAT FIRST JOB

1. **GETTING THAT FIRST JOB IS 80% LUCK**—20% CREDENTIALS.
   - LUCK IN THE SENSE THAT YOU AND A JOB YOU FIT HAPPEN TO BE IN THE SAME PLACE AT THE SAME TIME.
   - KEY IS PERSEVERANCE—KEEP AT IT.

2. **YOUR BIGGEST SINGLE ASSET IS GOOD NETWORKING.**
   - NETWORKING—KNOWING PEOPLE WHO KNOW PEOPLE AND USING THOSE CONTACTS. MOST OF YOU WON'T HAVE A NETWORK NOW, BUT START WORKING ON IT. HOW?
   - BE VISIBLE WITH YOUR PEERS AND BUILD A STRONG PROFESSIONAL REPUTATION. YOU WANT TO BE "KNOWN"—FOR YOUR WORK AND YOUR ACCOMPLISHMENTS.
   - JOIN THE REQUISITE PROFESSIONAL ORGANIZATIONS (PRSSA, ETC.), ATTEND THE MEETINGS, AND *NETWORK*. WRITE FOR THE PROFESSIONAL JOURNALS OR TRY STORIES FOR THE LOCAL NEWSPAPER OR THE SCHOOL NEWSPAPER. PRACTICE YOUR PRESENTATION SKILLS BY BEING AVAILABLE FOR SEMINARS OR CLASSES OF PR STUDENTS.

3. **RESUMES.**
   - KEEP THEM TO ONE PAGE.
   - TRY TO EMPHASIZE HOW YOU CAN ADD VALUE TO THE ORGANIZATION YOU'RE APPROACHING RATHER THAN EMPHASIZING YOUR "OBJECTIVES."
   - RESEARCH THE ORGANIZATION YOU'RE APPROACHING AND TAILOR YOUR RESUME FOR IT—I.E., HIGHLIGHT THE EXPERIENCE OR TALENTS YOU HAVE THAT MIGHT BE PARTICULARLY APPLICABLE TO THE TARGET.

4. **WRITE A GOOD COVER LETTER.**
   - THE COVER LETTER IS AS IMPORTANT AS THE RESUME, PROBABLY MORE IMPORTANT.
   - KEEP IT SHORT, BUT EXPLAIN WHY YOU WANT TO WORK FOR THE PARTICULAR ORGANIZATION AND HOW YOU THINK YOUR SKILLS AND EXPERIENCE CAN HELP ITS EFFORTS.
   - DON'T PUFF UP EITHER THE LETTER OR THE RESUME. KEEP THEM FACTUAL AND SUPPORTABLE.
   - MAKE SURE BOTH THE LETTER AND THE RESUME ARE ERROR FREE. PUNCTUATION, SPELLING, GRAMMAR, FACTS, AND WORD CHOICE MUST BE ABSOLUTELY PERFECT. IF YOU CAN'T GET THESE RIGHT, WHY WOULD ANYONE EXPECT YOU COULD GET THE OTHER STUFF RIGHT?

5. **PICK YOUR TARGET.**
   - SELECT THE COMPANIES OR AGENCIES YOU THINK YOU'D LIKE TO WORK FOR AND RESEARCH THEM. ON-LINE RESEARCH WILL GET THIS FOR YOU AND/OR THERE ARE A NUMBER OF REFERENCES IN THE LIBRARY—THE FORTUNE 1000 LIST, THE LOCAL CHAMBERS OF COMMERCE MEMBERS LISTINGS, ETC. FOR AGENCIES, TRY THE PRSA BLUEBOOK OR ANY OF THE VARIOUS O'DWYER'S DIRECTORIES OF CORPORATE PR.
   - FIND OUT WHO THE PR DIRECTOR IS, I.E., THE BOSS. AT COMPANIES IT'S THE PR DIRECTOR. AT AGENCIES, IT'S THE MANAGER. (A SIMPLE PHONE CALL WILL GET IT FOR YOU).
   - SEND YOUR RESUME AND COVER LETTER DIRECTLY TO HIM OR HER. IF YOU KNOW SOMEONE IN THE ORGANIZATION, ALSO SEND AN FYI COPY TO HIM/HER. EVERY CONTACT HELPS.
   - SEND ANOTHER COPY TO THE HR OR PERSONNEL HEAD WITH A COVER LETTER SAYING YOU'VE ALSO SENT A COPY TO THE PR HEAD. YOU DON'T WANT TO RUFFLE FEATHERS BY APPEARING TO BE GOING AROUND ANYONE.
   - ALSO RESEARCH SMALLER COMPANIES IN THE AREAS IN WHICH YOU THINK YOU MIGHT LIKE TO WORK—COMPANIES UNLIKELY TO HAVE A PR STAFF (The Public Relations Bluebook should identify this for you . . . if there's no PRSA member for the company, there is a chance there is no PR pro working there).
   - GO DIRECTLY TO THE IDENTIFIED CONTACT WITH A LETTER AND RESUME SAYING IN EFFECT THAT YOU THINK YOU HAVE A SKILL THAT CAN HELP THEM, EXPLAIN WHY AND ASK FOR THE OPPORTUNITY TO MEET AND TALK ABOUT IT.

6. **INTERNSHIPS.**
   - THOSE OF YOU LOOKING FOR INTERNSHIPS SHOULD FOLLOW THE SAME PROCEDURE.

7. **MAIL A LOT OF LETTERS.**
   - BUT DON'T ASK FOR "INFORMATIONAL INTERVIEWS." YOU WANT A JOB, NOT CONVERSATION AND THE PEOPLE WHO CAN GIVE YOU A JOB ARE TOO BUSY TO CHAT IDLY.

8. **WHAT'S IN DEMAND?**
   - PEOPLE WITH GOOD RECORDS FROM SCHOOLS WITH SOLID PROGRAMS OF PUBLIC RELATIONS EDUCATION.
   - PEOPLE WITH EXPERIENCE FROM MEANINGFUL INTERNSHIPS.
   - PEOPLE WHO CAN WRITE WELL.
   - PEOPLE WHO HAVE INITIATIVE AND HIGH ENERGY.
   - PEOPLE WHO UNDERSTAND THE MEDIA AND HOW IT WORKS.
   - PEOPLE WHO ARE SELF-CONFIDENT AND ARTICULATE, BUT WHO HAVE THEIR EGO IN HAND.
   - PEOPLE WHO ARE SMART ENOUGH TO DRESS APPROPRIATE TO THE ENVIRONMENT AND WHO CAN DEMONSTRATE THEY UNDERSTAND WHAT MANNERS ARE.
   - PEOPLE WHO HANDLE THEMSELVES WELL ENOUGH TO BE SENT IN UNESCORTED TO MIDDLE MANAGERS WITH CONFIDENCE THEY'LL MAKE THE RIGHT IMPRESSION AND GET THE RIGHT INFO.
   - PEOPLE WHO GRASP COPY POINTS RAPIDLY, I.E., RECOGNIZE THE "STORY."

9. **WHAT'S IN FOR YOU?**
   - STARTING SALARIES FOR ENTRY LEVEL JOBS IN THIS AREA ARE IN THE $35,000 TO $45,000 RANGE.
   - CPRO'S FOR MAJOR CORPORATIONS TODAY ARE EARNING IN THE HIGH SIX FIGURES AND MANY, WITH STOCK OPTIONS, ARE WELL ABOVE THE SEVEN FIGURE MARK. BY THE TIME YOU GET TO THAT STAGE, THE EARNINGS POTENTIAL OUGHT TO BE VERY, VERY ATTRACTIVE.
   - BESIDES, IT'S THE BEST GAME IN TOWN . . . THE MOST EXCITING, MOST REWARDING, MOST CHALLENGING GAME AROUND. WHO WOULD WANT LESS?
   - GOOD LUCK AND GOOD HUNTING.

#

INTERACTIVE EXERCISES CHAPTER 19

Writing Speeches

Exercise One

The chapter details the four fundamental steps in constructing a speech. As the head of the ISC PR department, you assign the first draft to one of your staff who has never written a speech. Write the paragraph you'd use in your memo to this staffer, explaining the key elements of good speechwriting.

Exercise Two

What are the essential details you need in making a decision whether or not to accept a speaking invitation? Again, write a short paragraph as if it is part of a general memo to your staff, explaining your criteria for deciding on speech-making opportunities.

Exercise Three

Write the opening for the speech by The Iowa Seed Company's marketing manager to the Austin Chapter of Future Farmers of America. Your objective is to position ISC as a strong supporter of the FFA, as well as to build good will that can be converted in marketing opportunities as FFA members graduate school and become active farmers.

Use the CD-ROM to check your responses.

## CHAPTER TWENTY

WRITING FOR THE INTERNAL CONSTITUENCY

Most organizations say their most important constituency is either their customers or their shareholders, or both. Though these are dominantly powerful constituencies, they are not the most important.

Their most important constituency is their employees.

If employees don't turn out good products or give good service, if they loaf or are wasteful, if they don't take pride in their work or cooperate with management, then quality suffers. When quality is poor, productivity falls, customers are unhappy, sales lag and shareholders watch their stock price erode. Organizations with unhappy customers and dissatisfied stakeholders do not survive long.

This is true whether the organization is an auto manufacturer, a dot.com, a hospital or a retailer. If employees do not perform well, bad things happen.

One technique organizations use to enlist support from employees is through an organized program of targeted and direct communications.

SLICK MAGAZINES TO SIMPLE LETTERS

Any tool that can be used for communicating to other constituencies is a tool that should be considered, and used where appropriate, with employee audiences.

The objective of the writing for internal audiences remains the same as with other areas: you want to make something happen.

In this case, the objective is to help create buy-in. You want to keep employees informed on the actions and objectives of the organization, help them see and understand how their attitudes and actions fit into the overall scheme, and generate their support and involvement. Employees must understand how working together benefits everyone.

CREDIBILITY AND CONFIDENCE

To achieve this, the internal communications effort must be credible. It must inform. It must educate. It must take employees into management's confidence and let them know what's going on. It must explain actions and in-action and whether the results of either are good or bad for the organization and the employee. Effective internal communications efforts must absolutely level with employees to the degree permitted by competitive concerns, disclosure rules and confidentiality.

THE "BUT . . ."

The "but" in this case is that writing for internal audiences needs to be conversational and personal. And not only conversational and personal, but: straightforward, no pretensions, no hedging, no talking down, no propagandizing, and absolutely solid.

If it isn't seen as credible, it's worse than having no communication at all.

Credibility, however, is a very tricky matter and takes time and patience to build. Sadly, it takes very little time to tear down.

Nothing communicates better than reality. Talking the talk will make no difference at all, if you're not also walking the walk.

OF FUNDAMENTAL IMPORTANCE

For many years, the internal communications function was not among the more highly valued operations within organizations. The tool was thought to be useful principally to try to build the idea of "family" within the company. Much of the resulting communication was devoted to births and bowling scores. There was very little focus on the substance of the business or its problems and opportunities.

Given the ephemeral nature of employment in the new millennium and the erosion of the probability that anyone is likely to spend his or her working career at a single firm, the organization as "family" is no longer a very saleable concept. Today, what people want and need is solid information about what's going on with matters that affect their jobs. Bowling scores and births do not rate very highly on that scale. Straightforward information about operating problems and opportunities does.

The very uncertain and constantly changing social and economic environment of the 21st century means that managers can no longer operate under the old rules of command and control. Instead, they must rely on consent and consensus. They must have buy-in. Effective internal communication is the key to that effort.

Responsibility for the internal communications function is determined by the organization's structure. Traditionally, it was the province of the human resources or employee relations departments. This has changed in recent years, with most of the portfolio going to the public relations department. Public relations staffers generally have the writing skills, experience with various media, and knowledge of the organization's plans and goals that allow for effective communication with employees. In these cases, the human resources or personnel department retains the benefits communication responsibility, which has technical considerations and legal reporting requirements best suited to that discipline.

PACKAGES: THE INTRANET

Increasingly, the vehicle of choice for delivering important information to employees is the intranet. It is fast. It is direct. It can be accessed by the employee at the time most convenient to him or her. Some organizations post full-scale weekly employee newsletters, complete with headlines, graphic displays, story summaries and links similar to those found on the Web sites of major daily newspapers. Full-time staff members are assigned to the task. This staff concentrates on knowing its audience and recasting news and information being released to the public into copy that focuses on employee interests or concerns. They do original reportage covering matters of specific interest to employees, ranging from benefit program changes to personnel moves and new sales or fund-raising initiatives. They also serve as a two-way communications conduit, helping keep tabs on employee concerns or problems and relaying them to management.

The standard techniques of news and news-feature writing are used to produce the material carried on these intranet sites. Remember, the emphasis is on brevity and is similar to the *USA Today* approach of bold headlines and short copy, but different in that the tone is informal and sometimes even chatty. Longer pieces are featured when an important issue needs to be discussed or a major development announced.

Organizations also use their intranet to get breaking news to employees at the same time it is being released to the media, so employees receive word before they see it in the local newspaper or hear it on the evening news. In these cases, the usual procedure is to post an actual copy of the release on the intranet at the same time it is being released to the media, preceded by an alert announcing that a special news release is coming.

PACKAGES: NEWSLETTERS AND LETTERS

Newsletters are also done in printed form, appearing weekly or monthly. Most don't have the graphic zing of an intranet piece (though some do). They are usually done in an 8 1/2″ by 11″ format, printed front to back on a single sheet using the same *USA Today* style that dominates intranet writing.

Sometimes, the only formal device is a simple letter to all employees from the boss, when there is something important to communicate. These typically have a very personal tone and are written as if the boss is talking directly to the employee, taking him or her into her confidence and getting an important matter across in a straightforward way.

Employee newsletters don't need to be elaborate to be effective. Sometimes very simple and straightforward approaches have more impact. To follow is an example of such a newsletter. It is plain and simple and devotes itself to only one topic—the progress on a major changeover the company has underway. The language is uncomplicated. The message is direct. It works.

Conversion date:
March 31, 2005

Days left until conversion:
175

Core system Project Update

Keeping you in touch and informed
Issue # 05   October 04, 2004

New Imaging System Gets Rave Reviews

Last week we completed training on our new imaging system. For reactions to the training and the potential of our new imaging system, a few of our trainees had this to say:

"It's going help us organization-wide because we don't have to pull documents from the files anymore, especially for the branches," noted Jennifer Lieu, Walnut Creek Sales & Service. "They won't have to wait for us to find the document then fax it to them. I also think it's great that the equipment brings us up to date with getting rid of paper – the less paper the better."

"At first it appeared complicated," Dennis Potts, our Fresno Branch Manager said. "But once you learn the system it is logical and user-friendly. It's going to be *sooooo* cool! Just the amount of time savings will be impressive since everyone has access to the images regardless of where they are physically located. We will all have instant access to signature cards, driver's licenses, loan documents, etc. – the whole enchilada."

"The imaging system will be a great tool for us," Lisa Shaffer of Consumer Lending stated. "It will make life easier for us in finding documents and eliminating all that filing. I especially like the fact that, because it is linked to our data base host, it reduces our margin of error when working with member accounts. It helps eliminate errors by filling in information like a member's name and social security number when all you have is the account number. The images are clear and the system is user-friendly."

Conversion Project Dates of Note

2004			2005	
Oct.	18 to 22:	Symitar here Parameters	Feb. 15:	On-site teller training begins
Nov.		TSG and Accounting training	Mar. 31:	Last day on Summit system
Dec.		Mini-conversion	Apr. 01 to 03:	Conversion weekend CU closed to members on Friday, April 01
			Apr. 04:	Live on new Symitar system

PACKAGES: MAGAZINES AND VIDEO

Other tools include full-color monthly or quarterly magazines devoted exclusively to the interests of employees and their families, or monthly newspapers in broad-sheet or tabloid format. It's also effective to regularly produce newsmagazine-style television for viewing at employee meetings, on a continuous running loop in office locations, or mailed to an employee's home to be watched with his or her family.

The magazine writing is almost all done in feature style; newspaper writing is done through a combination of news and feature styles.

Writing for the video presentation depends on the show's format and is usually assigned to people with experience in that form.

Magazines targeted to employees can rival the best of the big consumer and business publications in graphics and excellence of writing. Chevron/Texaco's employee magazine falls within that category. The following is a magazine spread that has all the appeal of a big consumer magazine layout. It gets an important story across to employees with style and impact.

ANGOLA SPECIAL REPORT

From the ground up

BY NANCY BOAS

By helping relaunch farming in Angola's fertile interior and by supporting other economic development, ChevronTexaco's Angola Partnership Initiative and partners hope to jump-start the nation's economic recovery. Here, farmers prepare soil for cultivation.

The Angola Partnership Initiative aims to help reconstruct a nation's economy. For ChevronTexaco and its international lineup of development partners, it's an unprecedented proposal.

THINGS GROW FAST AT THE EDGE OF RUBBISH heaps. The thought struck Lothe Sapuile like a lightning bolt. He was staring at weeds bursting from garbage mounds at the sprawling San Pedro marketplace in the Huambo province, high in Angola's fertile Planalto region.

The third-generation farmer was struggling to grow corn for seed on his 741 acres (300 hectares), a two-hour drive away on rutted rollercoaster roads still surrounded by land mines. Like all farmers throughout these highlands,

Sapuile had little cash, equipment or fertilizer. Those things had disappeared during Angola's 27 years of civil war. Without fertilizer, Sapuile's seed yield would be as depleted as his soils.

Producing seed was important — for Sapuile and two-thirds of the Angolan population. When peace took hold in early 2002, thousands of displaced men and women poured into the Planalto region, hoping to survive by farming even the smallest of patches. War had isolated Planalto from the rest of the world,

For French and Portuguese translations of this article, please visit our Web site: www.chevrontexaco.com/news/publications/.

Pour obtenir une traduction en français de cet article, veuillez visiter notre site Web à l'adresse: www.chevrontexaco.com/news/publications/.

Para a tradução em português deste arquivo, por favor visite nosso Web site em: www.chevrontexaco.com/news/publications/.

The internal communications portfolio also includes writing the presentations and scripting the remarks to be used at employee meetings, giving as much care and emphasis to their preparation as to remarks for any key external audience.

Any, and all, tools that can be used for mass or interpersonal communications are the province of the internal communications writer.

The keys to the success of the effort are:

· Candor—tell it like it is.
· Clarity—keep it as simple and uncomplicated as possible.
· Timeliness—tell it as rapidly as you can and don't let employees get the important information from the media before they get it from you.
· Relevance—make sure the information is important to the employee's situation and interests.
· Respect—give proper regard to the employee's intelligence and value his or her importance to the organization.

The writing challenges inherent with the internal communications portfolio are perhaps broader than any other single area of public relations writing. In many cases the writer doesn't have the luxury of fashioning different pieces to fit different audiences. Most frequently, she is writing for a diverse workforce that can range from Ph.D. level scientists to lawn maintenance workers. Crafting a single piece that works for all takes real talent.

INTERACTIVE EXERCISES CHAPTER 20

Writing for the Internal Constituency

Exercise One
Does the Fwsh apply to internal communications? If it does, take the Moore Foundation story (below) and apply the Fwsh to it as part of an internal communications initiative to create buy-in.

New Initiative Aimed at Crisis in Nursing

FOR IMMEDIATE RELEASE

CONTACT: Genny Biggs
Gordon and Betty Moore Foundation
Phone: 415-561-7722

San Francisco, November 19—The Board of the Gordon and Betty Moore Foundation announced today the approval of a 10-year, $110 million Betty Irene Moore Nursing Initiative to improve the quality of nursing-related patient care in five counties of the San Francisco Bay Area. The effort will be focused in Alameda, Marin, San Francisco, San Mateo and Santa Clara counties.

The Foundation will address the crisis in nursing care by funding projects to increase the quantity of registered nurses (RNs) in the San Francisco Bay Area and improve clinical skills effectiveness. "Quality of care for hospital patients is threatened as the shortage of nurses progressively worsens," said Betty Moore, co-founder and member of the Board of Directors. "If left unaddressed, these issues will become a severe public health problem."

"We hope to have a substantial and lasting impact on nursing-related patient care in acute care hospitals, as measured by improved patient outcomes," said Ed Penhoet, chief program officer for Science and Higher Education.

The Foundation will fund projects to increase the number of experienced, qualified RNs and expand the number of available training programs in the Bay Area. According to the American Hospital Association, nurses represent the largest healthcare workforce and provide approximately 95 percent of patient care in the hospitals, but the United States currently faces a shortage of more than 126,000 RNs. The Bureau of Labor Statistics projects a shortfall of approximately one million RNs by 2010. The field of nursing has been challenged by the rapid pace of developments in medical technology. Shortened patient stays, greater disease complexity, and more acute illness in the aging patient population compound this situation.

The portfolio of grants that constitutes the Betty Irene Moore Nursing Initiative is designed to have a synergistic impact on improving nursing care by addressing both the shortage of nurses and the need for more RN training in medical technology and treatment. In keeping with the Foundation's emphasis on the measurability of its grant making effectiveness, staff will compare changes in patient outcomes related to nursing care such as adverse events, complications, and patient and family satisfaction.

#

Exercise Two
What's the objective of a good internal communications program? Write a short paragraph explaining.

Exercise Three
Now write a two-paragraph story for the Moore Foundation employee intranet, using the information in the story above.

Use the CD-ROM to check your responses.

ET CETERA: SPECIAL WORDS AND SPECIAL READINGS

JARGON

All professions have their peculiar jargon, or language and terms which are understood by members of the group but aren't necessarily intelligible to the un-initiated. Below you'll find jargon used in the public relations profession and the meanings, just in case.

Audience—Recipients of a message; those targeted by a public relations program.

B-roll—generic film or tape used to illustrate a television story. Does not carry narration.

"Bank Account of Good Will"—Favorable opinion generated by a public relations program or other customer service campaign. A company may draw on its "Bank Account of Good Will" in difficult times.

Campaign—Strategic program designed to inform, convince, persuade or alter opinions on a particular subject.

Caps, Capital letters—Upper-case letters of the alphabet. Avoid using all-caps, as upper- and lower-case letters are easier for the eye to comprehend.

Commercial(s)—Advertisements for radio or television.

Contact—The person(s) listed on the news release as source of information. Can also mean a person or persons the media go to or information sources in general.

Copy—(noun) Written material.

Copy—(verb) To duplicate.

Coverage—Media time or space devoted to reportage on an event, cause, etc.

Deadline—Specific time or date for submission of information or completion of a project.

Draft—Working document, subject to editing.

Embargo—"Hold for Release"—used infrequently, with consent of reporter, who agrees not to use a story or information until a specified time. Releases "embargoed" are given to the news outlet in advance for release at a later time, as in "For Release no earlier than Tuesday, May 8 at 10:30 a.m.," or "HOLD FOR RELEASE: April 10."

Evergreen—Article "for the shelf," with no particular timeliness or urgency. Feature story that can be used any time.

Exclusive—Story given to one publication for its use alone.

File—(verb) To release. (noun) A place where information is stored.

Filler—Short blurbs, used to fill space in a publication.

Font—Type styles. Times Roman, Garamond and Century and a few others are recommended as being easy to read.

Format—General design or makeup of a publication, brochure or document.

Free-lancers—Writers or photographers who are not steadily employed by an organization but make their living by developing and writing stories or taking photographs for a variety of outlets.

Gatekeepers—Editors or news-directors who decide what will be published or aired, depending on the news value and/or time/space available.

Ghost writer—Someone who writes for another and is not identified as the author. Speeches, articles and manuscripts written for an employer or client may be "ghost written."

Glossy print—Shiny print of photograph. (See also: Matte Print)

Graf—Journalistic shorthand for "paragraph."

Graphic design—Art work, layout, etc.

Hook—The element of a story that grabs attention and holds interest.

Image—An individual's or group's perception of a person, product, project, company, organization, institution or cause.

Layout—Design for a publication, indicating where articles and art work or photography will be placed.

Lead—(pronounced: leed) First paragraph of a news, feature or opinion article, usually including some, if not all of the following: who, what, where, when, why and sometimes how.

Logo—Insignia of a company; identifiable graphic mark.

Matte print—Dull, not shiny, photographic print, suitable for use on television, as it does not reflect lights.

Media—Always plural, refers to print and broadcast channels. Medium is singular, used to mean one form.

Media kits—(also called press kits) Effective tools of the trade. Provided as resources for reporters and editors or other publics, these folders are often kept on file for future reference.

Move—The act of putting a release or story into public circulation, as in "move the release at 9:00 a.m."

NGO—Non-Government Organization (i.e., The World Bank, Hoover Institute, etc.)

News conference—(also called press conference) Meeting called to inform or explain event, news or issue to the media. Current preference is "News" Conference, because only print medium uses a "press."

News release—(also called Press Release) Article formatted for distribution to print and broadcast media. Current preference is "News" Release, since only print medium uses a "press."

Piece—A story, an article.

Pitch letter—A proposal for a story, sent to media.

Poll—Survey of specific group to determine preconceptions, attitudes or opinions.

Précis—(pronounced: pray-see) Essentially the same as a "pitch letter." Précis letters are used to sell story ideas to media.

Press conference (see News Conference)

Press kit (see Media Kit)

Press release (see News Release)

Promotion—Any special activity used to create awareness or interest in a person, product, project, organization or cause.

Publics—Groups of individuals, identified as targets for a public relations campaign.

Release—(noun) Article prepared for distribution to media.

Release—(verb) To issue information to media.

Reprint—Article or publication, duplicated for additional circulation.

Spot—A short message on radio or TV (usually 10–30 seconds) intended to sell a product or service or promote an event or an idea.

Target audience—Specific group or public to which messages or campaigns are directed.

Trade publications—Magazines and newsletters targeted specifically to particular professions, trades, causes or industries. (Examples: *The Strategist, Chemical Processing, Semiconductor Manufacturing,* etc.)

Wire services—National and international news-gathering organizations, such as Associated Press and Reuters, providing news to subscriber media.

SUGGESTED READINGS

Following are some suggestions on reading you might find worthwhile as you pursue this business of writing for public relations. Some demonstrate how really good writers handle things, some offer advice on nuts and bolts matters, and some intend purely to stimulate your thinking. Whatever time you care to invest in these readings will be time well spent.

1. *Literary Journalists*, edited by Norm Sims. A collection of features by masters of the craft—John McPhee, Joan Didion, Tom Wolfe, among others. This is the way it is done.
2. *The World's Great Speeches*, edited by Lewis Copeland and Lawrence Lamm. Examples of what the editors consider the best of the form, embracing all forms of oratory and showcasing many of the world's most memorable speeches.
3. *Words and Values*, by Peggy Rosenthal. "Dominant" words and how they direct actions and reactions.
4. *Writers on Writing*, edited by Robert Pack and Jay Parini. Most of the best advice about writing comes from writers themselves talking about what they do and how they do it.
5. *The Writers Chapbook*, collected from *The Paris Review*. A compendium of fact, opinion, wit and advice from some of the best.
6. *The Elements of Style*, by William Strunk and E. B. White. The classic.
7. *Eats, Shoots & Leaves*, by Lynne Truss. The zero tolerance approach to punctuation.
8. *Inside the Writer's Mind: Writing Narrative Journalism*, by Stephen G. Bloom
9. *The Journalist's Craft: A Guide to Writing Better Stories*, edited by Dennis Jackson and John Sweeney.

BIBLIOGRAPHY

Bernays, E. L. (1952). *Public relations.* Norman, OK: University of Oklahoma Press.

Bernstein, T. M. (1958). *Watch your language.* Great Neck, NY: Channel Press.

Center, A.H. and Jackson, P. (2003). *Public relations practices: Managerial case studies and problems.* Upper Saddle River, NJ: Prentice Hall.

Culbertson, H. M. and Chen, N. (Eds.) (1996). *International public relations: A comparative analysis.* Mahwah, NJ: Lawrence Erlbaum Associates, Publishers.

Cutlip, S., Center, A. and Broom, G. (2000). *Effective public relations.* Englewood Cliffs, NJ: Prentice Hall.

Fischer, J. (1976). "Public relations jargon." Unpublished manuscript. Columbus, OH: The Ohio State University.

Goldstein, N. (Ed.) (2002). *The Associated Press stylebook and briefing on media law.* Cambridge, MA: Perseus Publishing.

Gottschalk, J. A. (1993). *Crisis Response: Inside stories on managing image under siege.* Detroit, MI: Visible Ink Press.

Howard, C. M. and Mathews, W. K. (2000). *On deadline: Managing media relations.* Prospect Heights, IL: Waveland Press, Inc.

Hunt, T. and Grunig, J. E. (1994). *Public relations techniques.* Fort Worth, TX: Holt, Rinehart and Winston, Inc.

Marriott, J. W. Jr. and Brown, K. A. (1997). *The spirit to serve.* New York: HarperCollins Publishers, Inc.

McElreath, M. P. ((1997*). Managing systematic and ethical public relations campaigns.* Dubuque, IA: Brown & Benchmark Publishers.

Mencher, M. (2000). *News reporting and writing.* New York: McGraw-Hill.

Myer, V., Sebranek, P. and Van Rys, J. (2004). *Write for business.* Burlington, WI: UpWrite Press.

Newsom, D., VanSlyke Turk, J., Kruckeberg, D. (2000). *This is PR.* Belmont, CA: Wadsworth/Thomson Learning.

Newsom, D., Siegfried, T. (1981). *Writing in public relations practice.* Belmont, CA: Wadsworth Publishing Company.

Nolte, L. W. (1979). *Fundamentals of public relations: Professional guidelines, concepts and integrations.* New York: Pergamon Press.

Rayfield, R. E., Acharya, L., Pincus, J. D. and Silvis, D. E. (1991). *Public relations writing: Strategies and skills.* Dubuque, IA: Wm. C. Brown Publishers.

Regester, M. (1989). *Crisis management: What to do when the unthinkable happens.* Australia: Century Hutchinson.

Rhody, R. (1999). *The CEO's Playbook: Managing the outside forces that shape success.* Sacramento, CA: Academy Press.

Sabato, L. J. (2000). *Feeding frenzy: Attack journalism and American politics.* Baltimore, MD: Lanahan Publishers, Inc.

Seib, P. and Fitzpatrick, K. (1995). *Public relations ethics.* Fort Worth, TX: Harcourt Brace & Company

Seitel, F. P. (2004). *The practice of public relations.* Englewood Cliffs, NJ: Pearson Prentice Hall.

Sledd, J. (1959). *A short introduction to English grammar.* Chicago, IL: Scott, Foresman and Company.

Stahr, J. (1969). *Write to the point.* New York: The Macmillan Company.

Stone, B. and Jacobs, R. (2001). *Successful direct marketing methods.* New York: McGraw-Hill.

Truss, L. (2003). *Eats, Shoots & Leaves: The zero tolerance approach to punctuation.* New York: Gotham Books.

Tucker, K. and Derelian, D. (1989). *Public relations writing: A planned approach for creating results.* Englewood Cliffs, NJ: Prentice Hall.

Young, D. (1996). *Building your company's good name.* New York: American Management Association.

Wilcox, D. L., Cameron, G. T., Ault, P. H. and Agee, W. K. (2003). *Public relations: Strategies and tactics.* Boston: Allyn and Bacon

ABOUT THE AUTHORS

RON RHODY, APR, FEL

Ron Rhody heads The Rhody Consultancy which works with executives in business, academic and not-for-profit sectors on a wide range of internal and external communications and public relations issues.

Before forming TRC in 1993, he was Executive Vice President and Director, Corporate Communications and External Affairs, for BankAmerica Corporation and Bank of America NT&SA and a member of the corporation's Senior Management Council. At BankAmerica, he was responsible for the corporation's public relations and communications strategies, policies and programs during one of the most significant decades in its history.

Before joining BankAmerica, Rhody was Corporate Vice President and Director of Public Relations and Advertising for Kaiser Aluminum & Chemical Corporation. There he served on the corporation's managing committee and directed the communications strategies for the intense marketing battles and the international expansions and downsizings that were endemic to the world aluminum industry.

Prior to joining Kaiser, he worked as a daily newspaper reporter and editor, as a broadcast newsman and news director, and in state government in his native Kentucky.

Rhody was named Public Relations Professional of the Year by the professional journal, *Public Relations News;* received the Rex Harlow Award for outstanding professionalism; was selected as one of the top ten public relations professionals in the United States by *Public Relations Reporter;* received the International Association of Business Communicators Distinguished Communicator Award; gained the Lifetime Achievement Award of *Inside PR* Magazine; was elected to the Arthur W. Page Society Hall of Fame; is a Fellow (FEL) of the Public Relations Society of America, and is accredited (APR) by PRSA. He is the founding chairman of The San Francisco Academy, past chairman of the Public Relations Seminar, and has taught Writing for Public Relations as a guest lecturer at University of the Pacific in Stockton, Calif.

Rhody is the author of *the CEO's Playbook: Managing the Outside Forces That Shape Success*; "Public Relations and the Law" for the college text, *Public Relations Principles*; "Financial Public Relations" for *Lesley's Handbook of Public Relations and Communications*, and "Public Relations and the CEO" for the book, *Practical Public Affairs*.

He and his wife, Patsy, make their home in Walnut Creek, Calif.

CAROL ANN HACKLEY, PH.D., APR, FEL

Carol Ann Hackley is Professor of public relations in the Communication Department, University of the Pacific, Stockton, Calif. Previously, she taught on the faculties of University of Nebraska, University of Hawaii-Manoa, The Ohio State University, and The Washington Center's seminar program. She served the Navy League of the United States as National Vice President for Public Relations.

She is the former Director of Marketing and University Relations for the three campuses (San Francisco, Sacramento and Stockton) of University of the Pacific. Earlier in her career, she was Public Relations Director for Lincoln Unified School District, Stockton, Calif.; Associate Editor of the *California Highway Patrolman* magazine; Executive Director of Journalism Association of Ohio Schools and worked in the legislative bureau for the *Honolulu Star-Bulletin*, and Hawaii Newspaper Agency's Advertising Promotion department. Daniel J. Edelman appointed Hackley "Professor-In-Residence," to work in the San Francisco, Sydney, Australia and London, England offices of Edelman Public Relations Worldwide, while she was developing the International Public Relations major for Pacific.

She has received the Rex Harlow Award for outstanding public relations professionalism; Northern California PRSA Compass Award; National 1st Place for graphic/design from Printing Industries of America; PRSA, Hawaii Chapter's Koa Anvil, for "exceptional contribution to public relations and to the people of Hawaii," and University of the Pacific's Eberhardt Teacher/Scholar Award.

A 20-year member of Oakland/East Bay Chapter, Public Relations Society of America (PRSA), Hackley has served as President, National Assembly Delegate and Ethics Officer. She is accredited in public relations (APR) by PRSA and is a member of the College of Fellows (FEL). She is a contributing editor on the Editorial Board of *PR Quarterly* and serves on the Sacramento City College Foundation Board.

She is the author of "International Public Relations: The Need for Responsible Practice," a chapter in *Human Rights and Responsibilities: Communication Strategies among Nations and Peoples*; co-author of "Case Study: Wells Fargo," in *Successful Direct Marketing Methods* and "American Public Relations networking encounters China's guanxi," *Public Relations Quarterly*.

Hackley received her Master's and Ph.D. from The Ohio State University in Educational Policy and Leadership, and a B.A. in Language Arts Education from California State University, Sacramento.

She and her husband, T. Cole Hackley, reside in Stockton, Calif.

THANKS!

Gratefully, the authors wish to thank the students at University of the Pacific and California State University, Long Beach, who "tested" the book and whose feedback and enthusiastic response to its content and conversational style were instrumental in helping shape *WORDSMITHING*.

They are deeply appreciative of the editing by Kim Floyd, Public Relations Director for Matsu Borough School District, Palmer, Alaska; the proofreading, scanning of illustrations and general computer assistance of Alexis Louie, rising young PR star, and the fine-tuning and final formatting completion by Hans Chun, doctoral student and future professor.